NEW ZEALAND'S SOUTH ISLAND

ROAD TRIPS

This edition written and researched by

**Brett Atkinson, Sarah Bennett,
Peter Dragicevich and Lee Slater**

HOW TO USE THIS BOOK

Reviews

In the Destinations section:

All reviews are ordered in our authors' preference, starting with their most preferred option. Additionally:

Sights are arranged in the geographic order that we suggest you visit them and, within this order, by author preference.

Eating and Sleeping reviews are ordered by price range (budget, midrange, top end) and, within these ranges, by author preference.

Map Legend

Routes

	Trip Route
	Trip Detour
	Linked Trip
	Walk Route
	Tollway
	Freeway
	Primary
	Secondary
	Tertiary
	Lane
	Unsealed Road
✖	Plaza/Mall
	Steps
)= =	Tunnel
	Pedestrian Overpass
- - -	Walk Track/Path

Boundaries

— — —	International
- - - -	State/Province
⌒⌒⌒	Cliff

Hydrography

	River/Creek
	Intermittent River
	Swamp/Mangrove
	Canal
	Water
	Dry/Salt/ Intermittent Lake
	Glacier

Highway Markers

① Highway Marker

Trips

1	Trip Numbers
9	Trip Stop
🔂	Walking tour
🔁	Trip Detour

Population

✪	Capital (National)
◉	Capital (State/Province)
●	City/Large Town
●	Town/Village

Areas

	Beach
	Cemetery (Christian)
	Cemetery (Other)
	Park
	Forest
	Reservation
	Urban Area
	Sportsground

Transport

✈	Airport
⊶●⊷	Cable Car/ Funicular
Ⓟ	Parking
⊶Ⓡ⊷	Train/Railway
⊶Ⓣ⊷	Tram

Note: Not all symbols displayed above appear on the maps in this book

Symbols In This Book

✅	Top Tips	🍷	Food & Drink
🔗	Link Your Trips	🌳	Outdoors
📝	Tips from Locals	📷	Essential Photo
🔁	Trip Detour	🚶	Walking Tour
📖	History & Culture	✕	Eating
👪	Family	🛏	Sleeping

⊙	**Sights**	🛏	**Sleeping**
⛱	**Beaches**	✕	**Eating**
🏃	**Activities**	🍷	**Drinking**
🎓	**Courses**	☆	**Entertainment**
👆	**Tours**	🔒	**Shopping**
🎉	**Festivals & Events**	ℹ	**Information & Transport**

These symbols and abbreviations give vital information for each listing:

☎	Telephone number	🐾	Pet-friendly
☻	Opening hours	🚌	Bus
Ⓟ	Parking	⛴	Ferry
🚭	Nonsmoking	🚊	Tram
❄	Air-conditioning	🚆	Train
@	Internet access	apt	apartments
🛜	Wi-fi access	d	double rooms
🏊	Swimming pool	dm	dorm beds
🍴	Vegetarian selection	q	quad rooms
📖	English-language menu	r	rooms
👪	Family-friendly	s	single rooms
		ste	suites
		tr	triple rooms
		tw	twin rooms

View of Lake Te Anau (p113) from Mt Luxmore on the Kepler Track

CONTENTS

PLAN YOUR TRIP

Welcome to
New Zealand's South Island.......... 5

New Zealand's South Island
Map 6

New Zealand's South Island
Highlights 8

Christchurch City Guide.................10

Queenstown City Guide.................11

Need to Know...............................12

ROAD TRIPS

1 Sunshine &
Wine   5–7 Days   17

2 Kaikoura
Coast   3–4 Days   29

3 Southern Alps
Circuit   12–14 Days   37

4 Milford Sound
Majesty   3–4 Days   51

DESTINATIONS

Marlborough & Nelson...................64
Picton 64
Havelock.................................66

Blenheim.............................67
Kaikoura 70
Nelson 74
Moutere Hills........................ 77
Motueka 78
Christchurch & Canterbury 81
Christchurch 81
Waipara Valley 88
Arthur's Pass 89
Methven 90
Geraldine...........................91
Lake Tekapo 91
Aoraki/Mt Cook National Park.... 93
Queenstown & Wanaka................ 96
Queenstown 96
Wanaka.............................101
Makarora 105
Cromwell 106
The West Coast.....................108
Hokitika 108
Fox Glacier 110
Fiordland & Southland 113
Te Anau 113
Milford Sound......................116

DRIVING IN NZ 117

WELCOME TO
NEW ZEALAND'S SOUTH ISLAND

Welcome to one of the world's ultimate outdoor playgrounds, bursting with opportunities for adventure amid diverse and inspiring landscapes. Top-of-the-South neighbours, Marlborough and Nelson make for splendid road-trip country with an emphasis on sunshine and good times. The scenic drive along the Kaikoura Coast rewards with whale-watching and seals, plus swimming and surfing at pristine beaches. Head inland from Christchurch along the Southern Alps Circuit for stunning vistas of glaciers, Aoraki/Mt Cook and turquoise Lake Tekapo. The mountains, fiords, lakes and coastlines of New Zealand's deep south will not disappoint. The road from adventure capital Queenstown leads to spectacular Milford Sound in Fiordland National Park – one of the world's great remaining wildernesses.

NEW ZEALAND'S SOUTH ISLAND

1 Sunshine & Wine
A seductive blend of wineries, alfresco dining and gentle leisure pursuits. **5–7 DAYS**

2 Kaikoura Coast
Enjoy wine-tasting and whale-watching along the Pacific Coast. **3–4 DAYS**

Cape Farewell
Farewell Spit
Collingwood
Takaka
Golden Bay
Abel Tasman National Park
Tasman Bay
Motueka
Richmond
Nelson
Blenheim
Picton
Marlborough Sounds
WELLINGTON
Cook Strait
Cape Palliser

TASMAN SEA

Karamea

Westport
Murchison
St Arnaud
63
6
Nelson Lakes National Park
Hanmer Springs
70
Kaikoura
Kaikoura Peninsula
1

Punakaiki
Paparoa National Park
Reefton
7
Lewis Pass
Lake Brunner (Moana)
7
Pegasus Bay

Greymouth
Hokitika
Ross
Arthur's Pass
Arthur's Pass National Park
73
6
Whataroa

Southern Alps Circuit
A seriously grand tour taking in sublime scenery and stacks of sights.
12–14 DAYS

3

Milford Sound Majesty
Absorb magnificent lake, mountain and forest scenery.
3–4 DAYS

4

Christchurch
Lyttelton
Banks Peninsula
Akaroa

Canterbury Bight

Mt Arrowsmith (2795m)
Mt Hutt
Aoraki/Mt Cook. Methven
Ashburton

Franz Josef Glacier
Fox Glacier
Aoraki/Mt Cook (3754m)
Mt Cook Village
Westland Tai Poutini National Park
Aoraki/Mt Cook National Park
Lake Tekapo
Temuka
Timaru
Waimate
Oamaru

Palmerston
Otago Peninsula
Dunedin

Haast
Haast Pass
Jackson Bay
Mt Aspiring (3085m)
Lake Wanaka
Wanaka
Arrowtown
Cromwell
Alexandra
Twizel
Lake Pukaki

Lake Mahinerangi
Milton
Balclutha

Glenorchy
Queenstown
Lake Wakatipu
Lake Wanaka

Catlins Conservation Park
Chaslands Mistake

Lumsden
Gore

Milford Sound
George Sound
Fiordland National Park
Lake Te Anau
Te Anau
Manapouri
Lake Manapouri

Winton
Invercargill
Bluff
Oban

Tuatapere

Foveaux Strait

Stewart Island (Rakiura)
West Cape
Dusky Sound
Doubtful Sound

SOUTH PACIFIC OCEAN

0   100 km
0   50 miles

NEW ZEALAND'S SOUTH ISLAND
HIGHLIGHTS
★

MAIDEN OF MILFORD

Milford Sound (left) A collage of verdant cliffs and cobalt waters reveals the iconic Mitre Peak. See it on Trip **4**

Kaikoura (above) A great spot to take a boat tour or flight to see whales, dolphins and seals. Watch them on Trip **2**

Queenstown (right) Against a backdrop of jagged mountains and a snake-shaped lake, travellers can hike, bike or raft, then spend the evening enjoying cosmopolitan restaurants and bars. Hit it on Trips **3** **4**

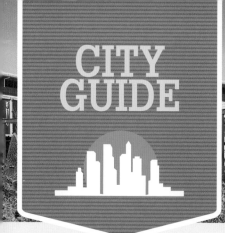

Above Shipping container cafe in Re:START Mall (p87)

CHRISTCHURCH

Christchurch is a vibrant city in transition, coping creatively with the aftermath of the 2010 and 2011 earthquakes. The city centre is graced by numerous notable arts institutions, the stunning Botanic Gardens and Hagley Park. Inner-city streets conceal art projects, pocket gardens and dynamic businesses repopulating the thinned-out cityscape.

Getting Around

Christchurch's flat topography and gridlike structure make getting around on foot or by bike a breeze. The extensive bus network (www.metroinfo.co.nz) is a cheap and convenient way of reaching the city's suburban attractions.

Parking

All-day parking is available throughout the city centre ($2 to $3.10 per hour), although roadworks and one-way systems may test your patience.

Where to Eat

While many cafes and restaurants still occupy the suburbs they fled to after the earthquakes – particularly around Addington, Riccarton, Merivale and Sumner – many new places are springing up in the CBD. Expect plenty of high-quality, exciting surprises, especially around Victoria St.

Where to Stay

As the rebuild progresses, more beds (for all budgets) are becoming available in the city centre and its inner fringes. If you're camping or touring in a campervan there are decent holiday parks within 20 minutes' drive of the city centre.

Useful Websites

Tourist Information (www.christchurchnz.com) Sights, accommodation, restaurants and events.

Neat Places (www.neatplaces.co.nz) Authoritative local blogger's views on the best of Christchurch.

Lonely Planet (www.lonelyplanet.com/christchurch) Destination low-down, hotels and traveller forum.

Trips Through Christchurch

Above Lake Wakatipu (p96) seen from the Remarkables

QUEENSTOWN

Framed by mountains and the meandering coves of Lake Wakatipu, Queenstown is a right show-off. It wears its 'Global Adventure Capital' crown with pride. The town's bamboozling array of adrenalised activities is bolstered by cosmopolitan restaurants galore, and excellent vineyards nearby. Boredom is definitely off the menu.

Getting Around

Queenstown's compact centre is easy to navigate on foot with the mountains and lakes allowing visitors to find their bearings. Connectabus (www.connectabus.com) has various colour-coded routes, reaching the suburbs and as far as Arrowtown.

Parking

There's plenty of cheap parking around the town but securing a space during busy times can be frustrating, especially near the lakefront. The Queenstown Lakes District Council website (www.qldc.govt.nz) shows car-park locations.

Where to Eat

The town centre is peppered with busy eateries. Many target the tourist dollar, but dig a little deeper and you'll discover local favourites covering a wide range of international cuisines. Reservations are recommended for the more popular places.

Where to Stay

Queenstown has endless accommodation options, but midpriced rooms are hard to come by. Hostels, however, are extremely competitive, and there are a couple of great holiday parks for campervanners. Places book out and prices rocket during the peak summer (Christmas to February) and ski (June to September) seasons; book well in advance.

Useful Websites

Tourist Information (www.queenstownnz.co.nz) Official Queenstown tourism website.

Queenstown i-SITE (www.queenstownisite.co.nz) Queenstown visitor information centre.

Trips Through Queenstown

NEED TO KNOW

MOBILE PHONES
European phones work on New Zealand's networks; most American or Japanese phones won't. Use roaming or a local prepaid SIM card.

INTERNET ACCESS
Wi-fi is available in most decent size towns and cities; sometimes free, sometimes hideously expensive. Internet cafes are few.

FUEL
Unleaded fuel (petrol, aka gasoline) is available from service stations across NZ, although be prepared in remote locations where there may be 100km between stations. Prices don't vary too much: per-litre costs at the time of research were around $1.80.

RENTAL CARS
Ace Rental Cars (www.acerentalcars.co.nz)

Apex Rentals (www.apexrentals.co.nz)

Go Rentals (www.gorentals.co.nz)

IMPORTANT NUMBERS
Country code (☏64)

Emergencies (☏111)

Climate

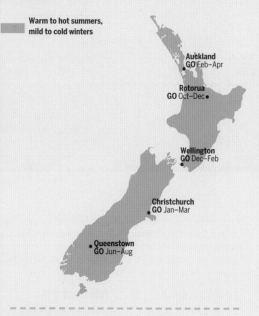

Warm to hot summers, mild to cold winters

Auckland
GO Feb–Apr

Rotorua
GO Oct–Dec

Wellington
GO Dec–Feb

Christchurch
GO Jan–Mar

Queenstown
GO Jun–Aug

When to Go

High Season (Dec–Feb)
» Summer: busy beaches, outdoor explorations, festivals and sporting events.

» Big-city accommodation prices rise.

» High season in ski towns and resorts is winter (June to August).

Shoulder Season (Mar–Apr & Sep–Nov)
» Prime travelling time: fine weather, short queues, kids in school and warm(ish) ocean.

» Long evenings sipping Kiwi wines and craft beers.

Low Season (May–Aug)
» Head for the slopes of the Southern Alps for some brilliant southern-hemisphere skiing.

» Few crowds, good accommodation deals and a seat in any restaurant.

» Warm-weather beach towns may be half asleep.

Daily Costs

Budget: Less than $150

» Dorm beds or campsites: $25–38 per night

» Main course in a budget eatery: less than $15

Midrange: $150–250

» Double room in a midrange hotel/motel: $120–200

» Main course in a midrange restaurant: $15–32

» Hire a car: from $30 per day

Top End: More than $250

» Double room in a top-end hotel: from $200

» Three-course meal in a classy restaurant: $80

» Scenic flight: from $210

Eating

Restaurants From cheap 'n' cheerful, to world-class showcasing NZ's top-notch ingredients.

Cafes Freshly roasted coffee, expert baristas, brunch-mad and family friendly.

Pubs & Bars All serve some kind of food, good and bad!

Vegetarians Well catered for, especially in cities and ethnic restaurants.

Price indicators for average cost of a main course:

$	less than $15
$$	$15–32
$$$	more than $32

Sleeping

Motels Most towns have decent, low-rise, midrange motels.

Holiday Parks Myriad options from tent sites to family units.

Hostels From party zones to family-friendly 'flashpackers'.

Hotels Range from small-town pubs to slick global-chain operations.

Price indicators for double room with bathroom in high season:

$	less than $120
$$	$120–200
$$$	more than $200

Arriving in New Zealand's South Island

Christchurch Airport

Rental Cars Major companies have desks at airport.

Buses Metro Red Bus (Nos 3 and 29) runs regularly into the city from 6.30am to 11pm; door-to-door shuttles run 24 hours.

Taxis To city centre around $50 (20 minutes).

Money

ATMs are available in all cities and most towns. Credit cards are accepted almost universally, although not American Express or Diners Club.

Tipping

Optional, but 10% for great service goes down well.

Useful Websites

Lonely Planet (www.lonelyplanet.com/new-zealand) Destination information, bookings, traveller forum and more.

100% Pure New Zealand (www.newzealand.com) Official tourism site.

Department of Conservation (www.doc.govt.nz) Essential information on national parks and reserves.

Te Ara (www.teara.govt.nz) Online NZ encyclopedia.

For more, see Driving in New Zealand (p117).

13

Road Trips

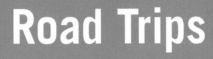

1 **Sunshine & Wine,** 5–7 Days
A seductive blend of wineries, alfresco dining and gentle leisure pursuits. (p17)

2 **Kaikoura Coast,** 3–4 Days
Enjoy wine tasting and whale-watching along the Pacific Coast. (p29)

3 **Southern Alps Circuit,** 12–14 Days
A seriously grand tour taking in sublime scenery and stacks of sights. (p37)

4 **Milford Sound Majesty,** 3–4 Days
Absorb magnificent lake, mountain and forest scenery en route to NZ's ultimate reveal. (p51)

Milford Sound (p60)
NICOLÁS CUERVO/500PX ©

Sunshine & Wine

This tour around the sunny top of the South Island serves up a seductive blend of wineries, alfresco dining and gentle leisure activities.

TRIP HIGHLIGHTS

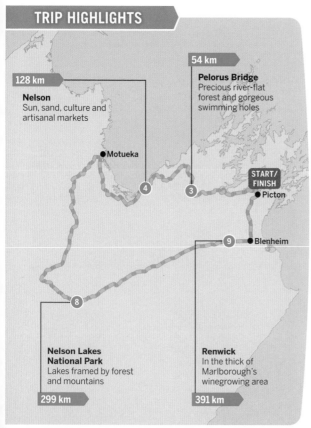

54 km

Pelorus Bridge
Precious river-flat forest and gorgeous swimming holes

128 km

Nelson
Sun, sand, culture and artisanal markets

●Motueka

START/FINISH
● Picton

●Blenheim

Nelson Lakes National Park
Lakes framed by forest and mountains

299 km

Renwick
In the thick of Marlborough's winegrowing area

391 km

**5–7 DAYS
432KM /
268 MILES**

GREAT FOR...

BEST TIME TO GO

November to March when the weather's best, but expect crowds during January.

 ESSENTIAL PHOTO

The jetty at Kerr Bay, Lake Rotoiti.

 BEST FOR WINE TOURS

Marlborough's world-class wines and unstuffy cellar doors.

1 Sunshine & Wine

Blenheim and Nelson vie annually for the crown of New Zealand's sunniest centre, so odds are on for blue skies on this trip around the top of the South. A high concentration of attractions and short driving times allow you to maximise enjoyment of outdoor adventures in hot spots such as Queen Charlotte Sound and Nelson Lakes National Park, as well as meander in a leisurely fashion around wineries and restaurants.

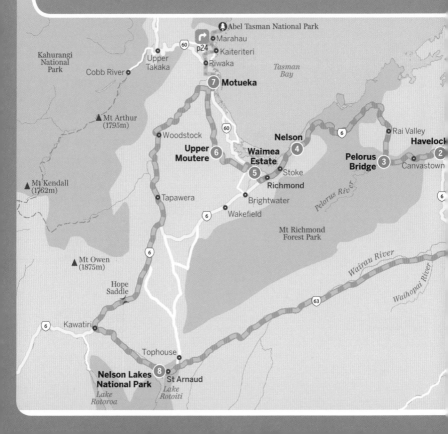

1 Picton (p64)

Spread around two pretty bays secreted deep within Queen Charlotte Sound, Picton is much more than just the inter-island ferry port and departure point for trips throughout the Marlborough Sounds.

The town and its environs can be surveyed from the popular **Snout Track** (three hours return), sidling along the Victoria Domain headland flanking the harbour's east side. A side track makes for a shorter walk to **Bob's Bay** (one hour return), which can be a good spot for a swim.

One of Picton's lesser-known but worthy attractions is the **Tirohanga Track**, a two-hour leg-stretching loop around a hill just behind the town. Taking you much higher than the Snout Track, it affords dress-circle views of the town and the endless ridges of the Sounds beyond.

The Drive » Follow signs for Queen Charlotte Dr, which winds around bay after bay for 34km through to Havelock, providing a panoramic Marlborough Sounds snapshot.

2 Havelock (p66)

The western bookend of Queen Charlotte Dr, the little town of Havelock is the hopping-off point for forays into Kenepuru and Pelorus Sounds.

It is also the self-proclaimed 'Greenshell Mussel Capital of the World'. You can familiarise yourself with this ubiquitous bivalve on the three-hour **Greenshell Mussel Cruise** (☎03-577 9997, 0800 990 800; www.marlboroughtourcompany.co.nz; Havelock Marina; adult/child $125/45; ☺departs 1.30pm), which provides a broad introduction to the Marlborough Sounds and, crucially, a sampling of steamed mussels and sauvignon blanc so you will be able to tick the region's ultimate wine and food match off your list.

Another attraction that might float your boat can be found inside the **Havelock i-SITE** (☎03-577 8080; www.pelorusnz.co.nz; 61 Main Rd; ☺9am-5pm summer only). This local information centre shares its home with the **Eyes On Nature** museum, a menagerie of frighteningly lifelike replica birds, fish and other critters. Colourful, fun and certainly surprising, it will be a hit with nature lovers of all ages.

The Drive » Follow SH6 west along the Pelorus River past the old gold-mining settlement of Canvastown and on to Pelorus Bridge, 20km away.

TRIP HIGHLIGHT

3 Pelorus Bridge

A peaky pocket of deep, green forest that is tucked between paddocks of pasture, the **Pelorus Bridge Scenic Reserve** (www.doc.govt.nz) contains one of the last stands of river-flat forest in Marlborough.

Waikawa

1 Picton

START/FINISH

Cloudy Bay

10 Blenheim

nwick

2

Awatere River

Seddon

Grassmere

Cape Campbell

Ward

0 — 20 km
0 — 10 miles

LINK YOUR TRIP

Kaikoura Coast

2 From Picton you can head down the east coast to Christchurch taking in more wineries and the odd whale along the way.

It survived only because a town planned in 1865 didn't get off the ground by 1912, by which time loggers' obliteration of surrounding forest made this little remnant look precious.

Explore the reserve's many tracks, admire the historic bridge, take a dip in the crystal-clear Pelorus River (alluring enough to star in Peter Jackson's *The Hobbit*), and then partake in some home baking at the cafe.

If you're travelling in a campervan or with a tent, consider overnighting here in DOC's small but perfectly formed **Pelorus Bridge Campground** (☑03-571 6019; www.doc.govt.nz; SH6; powered/unpowered sites per person $15/7.50), with its snazzy facilities building, lush lawns and riverside setting. Come sundown keep an eye out for long-tailed bats, known to Māori as pekapeka – the reserve is home to one of the last remaining populations in Marlborough.

The Drive » The 74km drive to Nelson along SH6 winds over the scenic Whangamoa hills. If you have a spare day, turn right 9km from Pelorus Bridge and head out to French Pass (or even D'Urville Island) for some big-picture framing of the outer Marlborough Sounds.

TRIP HIGHLIGHT

④ Nelson (p74)

Dishing up a winning combination of sandy beaches, parks and forest reserves, sophisticated art and culinary scenes, and lashings of sunshine, Nelson deserves its laurels as one of NZ's most liveable cities and a fulfilling holiday destination for visitors.

Nelson has an inordinate number of galleries, most of which are listed in the *Art & Crafts Nelson City* brochure (with walking-trail map) widely available around town. A particularly vibrant side of the city's creative scene is on show at the **World of WearableArt Museum** (WOW; ☑03-547 4573; www.wowcars.co.nz; 1 Cadillac Way; adult/child $24/10; ⊙10am-5pm), where you can ogle around 70 past entries of NZ's most inspiring fashion pageant. You name it, they've made a garment out of it: wood, metal, shells, cable ties, dried leaves, even ping-pong balls. Revel in sensory overload as you wander around the museum's galleries, including a glow-in-the-dark room, and the buxom 'Bizarre Bras' exhibition.

The Drive » Take the scenic route out of town via waterfront SH6, through Tahunanui and

MARLBOROUGH SOUNDS

The Marlborough Sounds are a scenic labyrinth of peaks, bays, beaches and watery reaches, formed when the sea flooded deep river valleys after the last ice age. They are very convoluted, accounting for almost one-fifth of NZ's total coastline.

Exploring the Sounds is invariably quicker by boat, with driving times up to three times longer. Accordingly, an armada of vessels offers scheduled and on-demand boat services, with the bulk operating out of Picton for the Queen Charlotte Sound, and some from Havelock for Kenepuru and Pelorus Sounds.

Indulgence combined with gentle recreation is a Queen Charlotte Sound speciality, with lunch cruises de rigueur. A fine choice is schmick **Bay of Many Coves Resort** (☑0800 579 9771, 03-579 9771; www.bayofmanycoves.co.nz; Bay of Many Coves; 1-/2-/3-bedroom apt $710/930/1100; ☎☒). Nestled into a secluded bay, it offers a dreamy one-stop shop of bushwalking, kayaking, swimming and a day spa, all on top of experiencing some of the region's best cuisine. You could do the whole shebang on a day trip, but luxurious all-mod-cons apartments overlooking the water make an overnighter pretty irresistible.

FOOD, GLORIOUS FOOD

Nelson's belt almost bursts with the weight of its restaurants and cafes, plumped up with fresh regional produce. Fortunately, visitors can readily source some for themselves from roadside stalls and regular markets.

The must-do on Saturday morning is a noodle through **Nelson Market** (📞03-546 6454; www.nelsonmarket.co.nz; Montgomery Sq; ⏰8am-1pm Sat). 'Bustling' ain't the half of it, so tightly packed is this weekly affair with fresh fruit and vegies, food stalls, artisan cheese and pickles, not to mention an array of art, craft and homespun fashions. Pork lovers should snuffle straight for Doris' caravan serving up the tastiest bratwurst outside the Mutterland.

The much smaller midweek **Farmers Market** (📞022 010 2776; www. nelsonfarmersmarket.org.nz; Morrison Sq, cnr Morrison & Hardy Sts; ⏰11am-4pm Wed) is an abundant alternative spruiking seasonal produce from asparagus to zucchini with bread, chocolate and other commendable edibles filling the gaps.

For a healthy blend of drinking, eating and exercise – with a super-sized helping of scenery on the side – hire a bike to ride the **Tasman's Great Taste Trail** (www. heartofbiking.org.nz). Mainly off-road and accessible from various points around Nelson and Motueka, this cycle route can easily be sliced and diced into an assortment of adventures.

Stoke, and alongside Waimea Inlet through to Richmond. Turn right on to SH60 to reach Waimea Estate, 16km from the centre of Nelson.

❺ Waimea Estate

Less of a global superstar than Marlborough, its behemoth, sauvignon-swirling neighbour, Nelson's wine region is quietly going about its business producing a variety of excellent drops including Old World–challenging pinot noir, chardonnay and riesling.

Waimea Estate (📞03-544 6385; www.waimea estates.co.nz; 59 Appleby Hwy, Richmond; ⏰10am-5pm Mon-Wed, to 9pm Thu-Sun) is a firm favourite for fine examples of these varietals as well as more adventurous drops like

Trev's Red, a plummy co-fermentation of three grape varieties, and the delightfully bright and quaffable albariño – a rare bird on these shores.

Pop in for one of the region's friendliest and most interesting wine tastings before retiring to the stylish conservatory or vine-view garden for a relaxed lunch of homemade pasta or local salmon.

The Drive » Continue along SH60 for 5km before turning left onto the inland Moutere Hwy. Traversing gently rolling countryside dotted with farms, orchards and lifestyle blocks, it's a scenic and fruitful drive, particularly in high summer when roadside stalls may be heaving with produce. Upper Moutere is 14km from the SH60 turn-off.

❻ Upper Moutere (p77)

Upper Moutere was first settled by German immigrants and originally named Sarau. Today it's a sleepy hamlet with a pretty church and a couple of shops, including the **Old Post Office** (📞03-543 2780; www.theoldpost office.co.nz; 1381 Moutere Hwy; ⏰9am-4pm Mon-Fri, 10am-4pm Sat & Sun), an endearing blend of micro-deli and cafe (stocking scrumptious local jam), with a gallery and gift shop on the side.

With jam in your bag, you're ready for a pint at the local pub. Reputedly NZ's oldest, complete with a questionably retro interior, the **Moutere Inn** (📞03-543 2759;

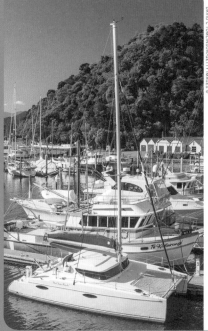

WHY THIS IS A CLASSIC TRIP
SARAH BENNETT, WRITER

This small but perfectly formed loop serves up so much that is good about NZ, starting – most importantly – with scenery from snowy mountains to sandy beaches and all sorts of other lovely landscapes in between. Add in blue skies, beach time, fine wine and juicy fruit, and you're getting pretty close to my holiday nirvana. But I would say that – I grew up here.

Top: Antipasto platter for wine tasting in Blenheim (p26)
Left: Picton marina (p19)
Right: Abel Tasman National Park (p24)

www.moutereinn.co.nz; 1406 Moutere Hwy) is a welcoming establishment serving honest meals ($13 to $20; homemade burgers, falafel salad) and local craft beer. Sit in the sunshine with a beer-tasting platter, or settle down on the sofa on folk-flavoured music nights.

Four kilometres from Upper Moutere, just off the highway to Motueka, bijou **Neudorf Vineyards** (☎03-543 2643; www. neudorf.co.nz; 138 Neudorf Rd; ⊙11am-5pm daily Oct-Apr, Mon-Fri only May, Jun & Sep, closed Jul & Aug) is one of the Nelson region's most celebrated wineries. Signature tipples include pinot noir and some of NZ's finest chardonnay, available to taste in the agriculturally chic cellar door.

The Drive » From Upper Moutere, continue north on the Moutere Hwy to its end 18km away at Motueka. In the distance, northwest of the town, you'll see the beech-forest-clad Mt Arthur in Kahurangi National Park.

- - - - - - - - - - - - - - -

❼ Motueka (p78)

Motueka (pronounced 'mott-oo-ecka' and meaning 'Island of Weka') is a bustling agricultural town that doubles as an ace visitor destination due to its ample accommodation, decent cafes and shops, and marginally salty setting along the shore of Tasman Bay.

The town's aerodrome gives rise to several hair-raising activities, including skydiving in one of NZ's most scenic drop-zones. **Skydive Abel Tasman** (☎03-528 4091, 0800 422 899; www.skydive.co.nz; Motueka Aerodrome, 60 College St; jumps 13,000/16,500ft $299/399) will spiral you up to 16,500ft and throw you out of a perfectly good plane strapped to a professional adrenaline junkie, at which point – if you can keep your eyes open – you'll see Abel Tasman, Nelson Lakes and Kahurangi National Parks, and as far away as the North Island.

Fancy the thrill without the spill? Skydive's front lawn is a lovely spot to spectate while soaking up some sun.

The Drive ≫ Motueka Valley Hwy is clearly signposted from the high street, heading down College St towards the aerodrome. Follow the highway 54km inland until its final juncture at SH6, turn right, and drive 39km to Kawatiri. Head left on SH63 following the Buller River to St Arnaud, 25km away. In all, this scenic drive into the mountains should take around 90 minutes.

- - - - - - - - - - - - -

TRIP HIGHLIGHT

⑧ Nelson Lakes National Park (p79)

Located at the northern end of the Southern Alps, Nelson Lakes National Park is a glacier-carved landscape of rugged greywacke mountains, ancient beech forest, and two stunning lakes – Rotoiti and Rotoroa ('small lake' and 'long lake'

respectively in Māori). St Arnaud, the tiny national park village, lies alongside the shore of Rotoiti.

The park's visitor hub is the **National Park Visitor Centre** (☎03-521 1806; www.doc.govt.nz; View Rd; ⊗8am-4.30pm, to 5pm in summer), well worth a visit for its informative displays on the park's ecology and history. It will also pay to call in to check the forecast and track conditions if you're venturing out onto the park's trails.

Changeable weather and tough terrain certainly make for some serious wilderness-hiking country, but numerous day walks offer more achievable options. Easy nature trails head off hither and zither from

DETOUR:
ABEL TASMAN NATIONAL PARK

Start: ❼ Motueka

Blanketing the coast and hill country between Tasman and Golden Bays, NZ's smallest national park is famed for its picture-perfect arcs of golden sand lapped by seas of shimmering blue. Slightly less likely to make the postcard rack are its myriad other natural features such as limpid lagoons, sculpted granite cliffs and gorges, and spectacular karst caves concealed in its rugged interior.

Hiking the **Abel Tasman Coast Track** is by far the most popular activity in the park, as is evident by the hordes that troop along it in high season. It's hardly a seething mass of humanity, however, with disadvantages limited largely to chock-a-block hut and campsite bookings, and the occasional risk of a photobomb.

Limit your exposure on a day trip. Boat cruises galore are offered from Kaiteriteri, the built-up holiday resort 16km from Motueka. If you're up for paddle power, however – arguably the best way to experience the park – bypass Kaiteriteri and head instead for Marahau, a mere 3km further away, where **Kahu Kayaks** (☎0800 300 101, 03-527 8300; www.kahukayaks.co.nz; 11 Marahau Valley Rd) can launch you on your way to glorious Anchorage beach from where you can walk south along the Coast Track back to base.

MARCO SIMONI/GETTY IMAGES ©

Kerr Bay jetty, Nelson Lakes National Park

Lake Rotoiti's **Kerr Bay**, offering a chance to smell sweet beech trees and eyeball the bird life. Reasonably fit walkers, however, should aim higher; a good pick is the five-hour **Mt Robert Circuit Track**, which circumnavigates the mountain, with an optional side trip along Robert Ridge offering staggering views into the heart of the national park.

The Drive » The 92km drive down the Wairau Valley to Renwick is pretty as a picture, complete with shingle peaks, a braided river, and golden paddocks that eventually give way to the endless rows of grapevines dominating the lower plains.

TRIP HIGHLIGHT

9 Renwick

Not so long ago an unremarkable dot, the little town of Renwick now occupies an enviable position at the centre of Marlborough's growing wine industry. An island in a sea of vines, with more than 20 cellar doors in its ambit – along with an increasing amount of accommodation and traveller services – it's a pleasant and convenient base for exploring NZ's premier wine country.

To cut straight to the wine chase, hire a bike from **Bike2Wine** (☎03-572 8458, 0800 653 262; www.bike2wine.co.nz; 9 Wilson St; standard/tandem per day $30/60, pickups from $10), whose friendly staff will happily advise on the best two-wheeled tour for your schedule, fitness and inclinations.

The Drive » Drive east on SH6 for 13km to Blenheim, passing Marlborough Airport after around 4km. If you can't see vines, vines, vines all the way after that, you're lost. Very lost.

MARLBOROUGH'S VINOUS COLOSSUS

Marlborough is NZ's vinous colossus, producing around three-quarters of the country's wine. At last count, there were 229 sq km of vines planted throughout the Wairau and Awatere Valleys – that's approximately 26,500 rugby pitches! Sunny days and cool nights create the perfect conditions for cool-climate grapes: world-famous sauvignon blanc, top-notch pinot noir, and notable chardonnay, riesling, gewürztraminer, pinot gris and bubbly.

Drifting between tasting rooms and dining among the vines is a quintessential South Island experience. Around 35 of Marlborough's 168 wineries have cellar doors, most open from around 10.30am till 4.30pm in summer (reduced hours in winter).

Contrary to rumours propagated by supermarket sauvignon blanc, Marlborough's terroir is extremely varied. To sniff out the interesting stuff hone in on smaller and independent wineries, rather than the big boys you recognise.

Picks of the bunch include **Framingham** (www.framingham.co.nz; 19 Conders Bend Rd, Renwick; ⊙10.30am-4.30pm), **Te Whare Ra** (www.twrwines.co.nz; 56 Anglesea St, Renwick; ⊙11am-4.30pm Mon-Fri, 12pm-4pm Sat & Sun Nov-Mar) and **Huia** (www.huiavineyards.com; 22 Boyces Rd, Blenheim; ⊙10am–5pm Oct-May). Two top-notch winery lunch options are **Rock Ferry** (☑03-579 6431; www.rockferry.co.nz; 80 Hammerichs Rd, Blenheim; mains $23-27; ⊙11.30am-3pm) and **Wairau River** (www.wairauriverwines.com; 11 Rapaura Rd; ⊙10am-5pm).

With ample parking and bike hire, the boutique **Vines Village** (www.thevinesvillage.co.nz; 193 Rapaura Rd; h10am-5pm) shopping centre, 5km north of Renwick, is a good place to get your bearings and collect the *Marlborough Wine Trail* map (www.wine-marlborough.co.nz). If you'd rather not drive, a host of wine-tour companies await to roll you around the traps, including long-standing **Highlight Wine Tours** (☑03-577 9046, 027 434 6451; www.highlightwinetours.co.nz).

⑩ Blenheim (p67)

Servicing the viticultural endeavours that carpet most of the Wairau Plains between the Wither Hills and Richmond Ranges, Blenheim is a bustling town with a fairly farmy, workaday feel. In recent years, however, town beautification projects and wine industry spin-offs (such as decent places to eat and pubs you can take your children to) are inching Blenheim closer to a fully fledged tourist town.

Threatening to blow the wine out of the water is the brilliant **Omaka Aviation Heritage Centre** (☑03-579 1305; www.omaka.org.nz; 79 Aerodrome Rd; adult/child $30/12, family from $45; ⊙9am-5pm Dec-Mar, 10am-4pm Apr-Nov). It houses a collection of original and replica Great War and WWII aircraft, brought to life in a series of lifelike dioramas (created by associates of *Lord of the Rings* director, Peter Jackson, who also owns the centre's Great War collection), depicting dramatic wartime scenes such as the demise of the Red Baron. Budding aces can take to the skies on vintage biplane flights.

The Drive ≫ Head north on SH1 for 28km to return to Picton. After leaving the wide Wairau Plains, the views narrow as you head up the Tuamarina Valley and past the Para Wetlands towards the Marlborough Sounds.

Right Marlborough vineyards

Kaikoura Coast

2

The inter-island ferry port of Picton and New Zealand's southern capital, Christchurch, are linked by a scenic highway wending through pretty countryside and along the wild Pacific Coast.

TRIP HIGHLIGHTS

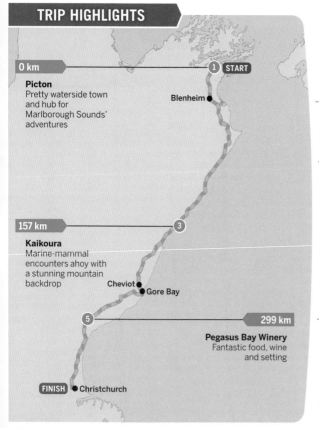

0 km

Picton
Pretty waterside town and hub for Marlborough Sounds' adventures

Blenheim

START

157 km

Kaikoura
Marine-mammal encounters ahoy with a stunning mountain backdrop

Cheviot

Gore Bay

299 km

Pegasus Bay Winery
Fantastic food, wine and setting

FINISH Christchurch

3–4 DAYS
352KM /
219 MILES

GREAT FOR...

BEST TIME TO GO

The scenery, wine and wildlife are great all year round.

 ESSENTIAL PHOTO

Queen Charlotte Sound snapped from the Snout Track.

 BEST FOR WILDLIFE

Kaikoura's ocean teems with dolphins, whales, seals and seabirds.

Left Gore Bay (p32)

29

2 Kaikoura Coast

This stretch of State Hwy 1 is a relatively quick and convenient route between the South Island's two major traveller gateways, Picton and Christchurch, but it also boasts several of the South Island's major highlights. The beautiful Marlborough Sounds, Blenheim's world-class wineries and Kaikoura's marine tours can hardly be missed, but hidden, low-key and up-and-coming attractions also abound.

TRIP HIGHLIGHT

① Picton (p64)

The inter-island ferry port town of Picton doubles as the departure point for adventures throughout the labyrinthine **Marlborough Sounds** (p20). Often overlooked, however, are Picton's many enjoyable adventures for landlubbers, including some great walks.

For an elevated perspective that makes the Sounds seem very much like the drowned valleys they are, follow the **Snout Track** (three hours return) along the headland flanking the harbour's east side. If

the short, sharp climb to the ridge line isn't quite what you had in mind, indulge in Picton's simplest and most popular activity, namely lolling about in the pretty foreshore park for a picnic, ice cream or fish and chips, and watch the comings and goings on both land and sea.

The Drive » Following SH1, it's only 28km to Blenheim through the Tuamarina River valley and Para Wetlands, then into the broad plains of the Wairau Valley.

② Blenheim (p67)

Approaching the town of Blenheim you'll be left in no doubt that you've entered wine country,

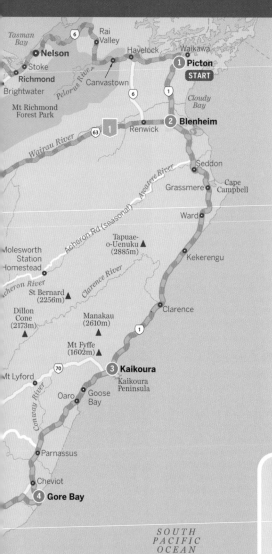

and fortunately it's easy to dip a toe into Marlborough's wine barrels without straying too far from the highway.

Just 3km off SH1, north of Blenheim, **Saint Clair** (www.saintclair.co.nz; 13 Selmes Rd, Rapaura; ⏱9am-5pm) is a long-standing, family-owned operation crafting some of NZ's most interesting and well-regarded wines, including the Pioneer Block range showcasing Marlborough's varied terroir. The adjacent cafe is an atmospheric spot for the obligatory vineyard lunch.

The good news for wine lovers is that the bulk of Marlborough's 35 or so cellar doors are scattered through the valley within a 15-minute drive. The **Vines Village** (www.thevinesvillage.co.nz; 193 Rapaura Rd; ⏱10am-5pm) is a good place to obtain a winery map and advice,

LINK YOUR TRIP

1 **Sunshine & Wine**

Starting in Picton and lopping around to Blenheim, this sunny route takes in the best of the top of the South.

3 **Southern Alps Circuit**

Christchurch is a common departure point for a grand tour of the mountainous south.

along with a bike if you'd rather wobble around on two wheels.

The Drive >> From Blenheim, SH1 cuts inland through Marlborough's second-largest grape-growing region, the Awatere Valley. Beyond the Clarence River, 88km from Blenheim, the peaks of the Seaward Kaikoura Range start to fill the picture, as does the spectacular coastline the road follows for much of the remaining 41km to Kaikoura.

- - - - - - - - - - - -

TRIP HIGHLIGHT

3 Kaikoura (p70)

Kaikoura is a pretty coastal town with a dramatic, snowy-peak backdrop. Its handsome peninsula is the place where – according to Māori legend – the demigod Māui placed his feet when he fished the North Island up from the depths.

Most people come here for marine tours, especially whale-watching, but the town also sports a particularly good walk. Starting from town, the three-to-four hour **Peninsula Walkway** is a mighty fine way to soak up the scenery, and offers the chance to see seals, shearwaters and other seabirds while learning about the area via a series of insightful information panels.

The walkway begins by following the town quay out to the peninsula's end, Point Kean, where seals laze around

seemingly oblivious to the attention of hordes of human gawpers. From there the pathway climbs gently to the top of limestone cliffs from where there are vast views in every direction. On reaching South Bay, the trail heads across the isthmus back towards the town.

The Drive >> SH1 hugs the coast, occasionally burrowing through odd tunnels in the rock, before climbing over the Hundalee Hills and heading down onto the bucolic Canterbury Plains. A 'Tourist Drive' signpost in the centre of Cheviot township directs you left down McQueen Rd to reach Gore Bay, 77km and a little over an hour from Kaikoura.

- - - - - - - - - - - -

4 Gore Bay

This is old-school NZ: aged beachside baches (holiday cottages), some dating back to 1865, and a long beach good for swimming and surfing. Gore Bay's permanent population of around a dozen people balloons in the summer, mainly with Kiwi campers, but any time of the year you'll still have plenty of sand to yourself.

Towards the northern end of the beach is a short track leading along the Jed River to a small, hilltop cemetery, containing just a handful of tombstones. It has lovely views of the wetland and beach, and is a peaceful

spot to enjoy the last of the day's sun.

Gore Bay is also known for its **Cathedral Cliffs**, which can be reached by car or a brutally steep 10-minute walk at the southern end of the village. Sculpted by wind and rain – in the evocatively named process known as badlands erosion – the clay gully walls resemble a cathe-

DAVID C TOMLINSON/GETTY IMAGES ©

Kaikoura

dral's organ pipes, also known as hoodoos.

The Drive >> Head south out of Gore Bay to complete the Gore Bay Tourist Drive, up and over the coastal hills to meet the braided Hurunui River, and soon hitting SH1 where you head south to Waipara. Total distance to Waipara is 59km.

TRIP HIGHLIGHT

⑤ Waipara Valley (p88)

Conveniently stretched along SH1 near the Hanmer Springs turn-off, this resolutely rural area makes for a mouthwatering pit stop en route to Christchurch. The valley's warm dry

summers and cool autumn nights have proved a winning formula for growing grapes. While it accounts for less than 3% of NZ's wine production, it's responsible for some of the country's finest cool-climate wines including riesling and pinot noir.

It's fitting that the Waipara Valley's premier

33

WHALE WORLD

Few places in the world are home to such a panoply of easily spottable marine wildlife. Whales, dolphins, NZ fur seals, penguins, shearwaters, petrels and several species of albatross all live in the Kaikoura area or swing by.

Marine animals converge here due to ocean-current and continental-shelf conditions: the seabed gradually slopes away from the land before plunging to more than 800m where the southerly current hits the continental shelf. This creates an upwelling of tasty nutrients from the ocean floor into the feeding zone.

Top-of-the-food-chain sperm whales congregate here all year round, but depending on the time of year you may also spy humpbacks, southern rights and even behemoth blue whales, the heaviest animals ever to have graced this earth.

With knowledgeable guides and fascinating 'world of whales' on-board animation, the town's biggest operator, **Whale Watch Kaikoura** (📞0800 655 121, 03-319 6767; www.whalewatch.co.nz; Railway Station; 3½hr tours adult/child $150/60), heads out on boat trips (with admirable frequency) to introduce you to some of the big fellas. It'll refund 80% of your fare if no whales are sighted (success rate: 95%), but if this trip is a must for you, allow a few days' flexibility in case the weather turns bad.

winery, **Pegasus Bay** (📞03-314 6869; www.pegasusbay.com; Stockgrove Rd; ⏰tastings 10am-5pm), should also have the loveliest setting and one of Canterbury's best restaurants. The beautiful gardens and sun-drenched lawn encourage a very long linger over contemporary cuisine and luscious wines; try the Canterbury lamb matched with Prima Donna pinot noir.

To fully indulge in the valley's bounty, pick up a copy of the *Waipara Valley Map* (www.waiparavalleynz.com). Otherwise, you'll spot several of the main players from the highway.

The Drive » Breaking out onto the Canterbury Plains south of Waipara, it's a flat and reasonably featureless 59km drive from Waipara to central Christchurch.

- - - - - - - - - - - -

❻ Christchurch (p81)

Christchurch is a city in transition, rebuilding from the 2010 and 2011 earthquakes that left 186 people dead and all but hollowed out the heart of the CBD.

While many historic buildings were destroyed, you can see architectural survivors as you walk around the city, including Canterbury Museum. Beautiful *pounamu* (greenstone) carvings can be found in its Māori galleries, while Christchurch St walks through the colonial past. The must-see is Fred & Myrtle's gloriously kitsch Paua Shell House – Kiwiana at its best.

The museum is also strong on natural history, but to see some of NZ's native animals in the flesh (or more likely feather), visit Willowbank Wildlife Reserve. As well as a rare opportunity to view kiwi, NZ's national bird, the reserve has a recreated Māori village where Ko Tane cultural performances are held in the evenings.

Right Fur seal, Kaikoura (p32)

Southern Alps Circuit

3

See a stack of the South's top sights on this trip along ceaselessly scenic alpine, coastal, lakeland and rural highways, dotted with towns ranging from rustic Ross to racy Queenstown.

TRIP HIGHLIGHTS

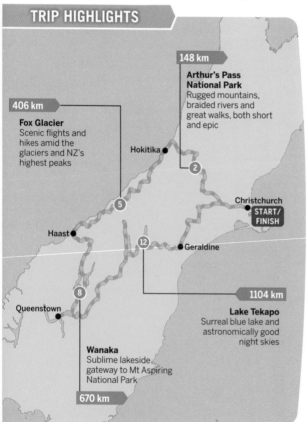

148 km

Arthur's Pass National Park
Rugged mountains, braided rivers and great walks, both short and epic

406 km

Fox Glacier
Scenic flights and hikes amid the glaciers and NZ's highest peaks

Hokitika

2

Christchurch
START/ FINISH

5

Haast

12

Geraldine

1104 km

Lake Tekapo
Surreal blue lake and astronomically good night skies

8

Queenstown

Wanaka
Sublime lakeside, gateway to Mt Aspiring National Park

670 km

**12–14 DAYS
1379KM /
857 MILES**

GREAT FOR...

BEST TIME TO GO
This is a stunner all year round.

 ESSENTIAL PHOTO
Lake Tekapo and the Mackenzie Country from Mt John's summit.

 BEST FOR MOUNTAIN SCENERY
An aerial sightseeing trip around Aoraki/Mt Cook.

Left Ice climbing in the Liebig Range, Southern Alps

37

3

Southern Alps Circuit

Nothing defines the South Island like the Southern Alps, the 500km-long series of ranges stretching from Nelson Lakes to Fiordland. This trip offers the chance to admire a vast swathe of them from all manner of angles on such quintessential New Zealand experiences as glacier ice hikes, scenic flights, cross-country bike rides and nature walks – or just staring out the car window, if you prefer.

① Christchurch (p81)

Nowhere in NZ is changing as fast as postearthquake Christchurch, and visiting the country's second-largest city during its rebuilding phase is both interesting and inspiring. What's more, the majority of Christchurch's prequake attractions are open for business, including the must-visit Canterbury Museum. Not only does it provide a well-rounded introduction to the city and region, it's also strong on the natural history of wider NZ.

Christchurch has long been a regular departure point for travellers to Antarctica. Near the airport (and serviced by a free shuttle from the central city), the **International Antarctic Centre** (☏ 0508 736 4846; www. iceberg.co.nz; 38 Orchard Rd, Christchurch Airport; adult/ child $39/19; ⊙ 9am-5.30pm) offers visitors the opportunity to learn about the icy continent, see live penguins, and experience -18°C wind chill in the storm chamber.

The Drive » Head out of the city limits on SH73, which strikes out across Canterbury Plains and heads into the Southern Alps. The Big Ben, Torlesse and Craigieburn Ranges are but a prelude to the mega-peaks of Arthur's Pass National Park, around two hours (148km) from Christchurch.

TRIP HIGHLIGHT

② Arthur's Pass National Park (p89)

Straddling the Southern Alps, Arthur's Pass National Park encompasses a seriously rugged landscape, riven with deep valleys and ranging in altitude from 245m at the Taramakau River to 2408m at the top of Mt Murchison. It's popular with alpinists and back-country trampers, but its dramatic wilderness can readily be appreciated on brief forays close to the highway.

There are multiple walking options from the village, including one of the best day hikes in the country. The strenuous climb up **Avalanche Peak** (7km, six to eight hours return) should only be attempted in fine weather by fit, well-equipped and experienced walkers. Those who do make the effort, however, will be rewarded with staggering views of the surrounding mountains, valleys and hanging glaciers.

The village itself, home to a permanent population of around 60, sports a couple of cafes and the **Arthur's Pass Visitor**

SOUTH
PACIFIC
OCEAN

Lake umner Forest Park
Hanmer Springs
Mt Lyford
Mt Longfellow (1898m)
ke mner
Waiau
Culverden
Waipara
Amberley
Pegasus Bay
ford
Woodend
Kaiapoi
START/ FINISH
① Christchurch
Rolleston Lyttelton
Lake Ellesmere
Akaroa
Banks Peninsula

LINK YOUR TRIP

② **Kaikoura Coast**
From Christchurch you can head up the east coast to Picton taking in more wineries and the odd whale along the way.

④ **Milford Sound Majesty**
Lakes, mountains and waterfalls decorate this super-scenic drive from Queenstown to Milford Sound via Te Anau.

Centre (☎03-318 9211; www.doc.govt.nz; 80 Main Rd; ⏰8.30pm-4.30pm). Pop in here for walking track information and local weather forecasts.

The Drive » Continue west on SH73. Beyond the pass (920m), mountain vistas give way to rural scenes as the highway winds down to meet SH6, the West Coast Rd. At Kumara Junction head south to Hokitika, 22km away for a total of 100km (around 90 minutes) driving.

③ Hokitika (p108)

Just one of scores of West Coast towns founded on gold, Hokitika boasts an admirable array of historic buildings, including the 1908 Carnegie Building housing the Hokitika Museum. An exemplary provincial museum and easily the best on the coast, its wide-ranging displays cover such topics as the gold rushes, the region's natural and social history, and traditional Māori use of *pounamu*.

Hokitika today is a stronghold of this indigenous and highly prized stone, judiciously gathered from nearby rivers. It is fashioned into pendants and other personal treasures by master carvers who jostle for position alongside jewellers, glass-blowers and various other crafts-people. Art-lovers will find the town a delight.

Keep your fingers crossed for a clear evening, because five minutes' walk from the town centre is **Sunset Point** – a primo place to watch the light fade with a feed of fish and chips, seagulls circling, and big Tasman Sea waves crashing on the driftwood-strewn shore.

The Drive » Just south of Hokitika are a couple of scenic walks – the historic Mananui Tramline, which has outstanding historical information panels, and the commercial Treetop Walkway, a canopy-level construction built from steel. The rest of the 27km drive to Ross cuts inland through a mixture of pasture and patches of forest.

④ Ross

Ross was the scene of a major kerfuffle in 1907 when NZ's largest gold nugget (the 2.772kg 'Honourable Roddy') was unearthed. The **Ross Goldfields Heritage Centre** (www.ross.org.nz; 4 Aylmer St; ⏰9am-4pm Dec-Mar, to 2pm Apr-Nov) displays a replica Roddy, along with a scale model of the town in its glittering years. Starting near the museum, the **Water Race Walk** (one hour return) passes old gold diggings, caves, tunnels and a cemetery.

Apparently there's still gold in them thar hills,

MĀORI GREENSTONE ROUTES

The South Island is known in Māori as Te Waipounamu – the waters of greenstone – which gives some idea of the stone's importance during the early days of Aotearoa's settlement. *Pounamu* (greenstone) is nephrite jade, bowenite or serpentinite, prized for its toughness and beauty and used to make weaponry, tools and jewellery.

Pounamu comes from only one place in New Zealand – the western side of the Southern Alps, particularly from rivers around Hokitika. It was the search for *pounamu* that saw Māori, from around AD 1300, forge routes from the more populated east coast through river valleys and over mountain passes. These were incredibly intrepid journeys through wild terrain made all the more frightening by NZ's volatile maritime climate. The navigational and survival skills of these Māori explorers were a boon for pioneering Europeans who relied heavily on their guidance when surveying the South during the 19th century.

Arthur's, Haast and Lewis Passes, Buller Gorge and the Milford Hwy – all were once single-track pathways followed by Māori greenstone gatherers. Others – such as Mackinnon Pass (on the Milford Track) and Harper Pass – have remained passable only on foot.

so you might like to try a spot of gold panning in Jones Creek. The $10 pan hire fee is a small outlay for the chance to find Roddy's great, great grandnuggets, don't you think?

Okay, maybe not. You could just spend the tenner on a pint at the **Empire Hotel** (☎03-755 4005; 19 Aylmer St). Established in 1866 and one of the West Coast's hidden gems, the bar (and many of its patrons) are testament to a bygone era. Breathe in the authenticity, along with a whiff of woodsmoke, over a beer and an honest meal.

The Drive ›› The 131km, two-hour drive south to Fox Glacier meanders inland crossing numerous mighty West Coast river systems, cutting through dense rainforest and passing tranquil lakes. The 30-minute section between Franz Josef Glacier and Fox Glacier townships will blow your socks off (if it's not raining...).

TRIP HIGHLIGHT

⑤ Fox Glacier (p110)

Fox Glacier is the smaller and quieter of the twin glacier townships, and is set in more rural surrounds. While you should linger in both if your itinerary allows, Fox is our pick of the two.

Fox's glacier viewing options are remarkably similar to those of Franz. Scenic helicopter flights are offered by a raft of operators touting for business on the main road. There is also a choice of independent or guided walks up into the glacier valley, as well as glacier hikes with Fox Glacier Guiding.

For a unique perspective of the glaciers, consider leaping out of a perfectly good plane above them. Skydive Fox Glacier offer tandem jumps from 13,000ft and 16,500ft. If you want to strike skydiving off your bucket list, you'd be hard pushed to find a more dramatic setting for it.

The Drive ›› Allow 90 minutes to reach Ship Creek, 103km away along a scenic stretch of highway chopped through lowland forest and occasional pasture with intermittent views seaward. Stop 5km south of Lake Moeraki at Knights Point, a spectacular lookout commemorating the opening of this stretch of highway in 1965.

⑥ Ship Creek

For a taste of the wilderness that qualifies the Haast region for inclusion in Te Wāhipounamu–South West New Zealand World Heritage Area, you can't go past Ship Creek. Well, you can, but you shouldn't.

The car park alongside the highway is the trailhead for two fascinating walks. We suggest starting with **Kahikatea Swamp Forest Walk**, a 20-minute amble through a weird bog, before heading on to the beach for the **Dune Lake Walk**. This salty, sandy amble is supposed to take half an hour but may well suck you into a vortex of beach-combing, wave-watching, seabird-spotting and perhaps even a spot of tree-hugging in the primeval forest around the reedy lake.

The Drive ›› SH7 sticks close to the coast before crossing the Haast River on NZ's longest single-lane bridge. At Haast Junction, around half an hour from Ship Creek, take SH6 to Haast township – a chance to

TOP TIP: PESKY SANDFLIES

You will encounter sandflies on the West Coast. While they don't carry diseases they are a pain in the bum, face, arm, leg, ankle or whatever else is exposed. Your best deterrent is to cover up, although effective DEET-free products such as Okarito Sandfly Repellent are also readily available. Thankfully sandflies do go to bed after dark, allowing you some respite!

DAVID WALL PHOTO/GETTY IMAGES ©

MARCO SIMON/ROBERTHARDING/GETTY IMAGES ©

WHY THIS IS A CLASSIC TRIP
SARAH BENNETT, WRITER

This loop is the premier NZ road trip – the first I suggest to anyone exploring for a couple of weeks or more. There are endless reasons why – especially when you factor in dozens of possible detours – but it's the chance to penetrate deep into the mountains via Arthur's and Haast Passes that makes it so memorable. Incredibly dramatic in themselves, they also gate-keep the mind-bendingly different landscapes either side of the alps.

Top: Hot-air balloon near Methven (p49)
Left: Tourists on Fox Glacier (p41)
Right: Blue Pools, near Makarora

stock up on food and fuel –
before continuing on towards
Haast Pass. This 97km leg will
take just under two hours.

- - - - - - - - - - - -

❼ Makarora (p105)

The first sign of life after
crossing Haast Pass into
Central Otago, middle-of-
nowhere Makarora sur-
vives as a road-trip stop
and a base for adventure
into Siberia.

No, not that Siberia.
We're talking about the
remote wilderness val-
ley within **Mt Aspiring
National Park**, reached
on one of the South
Island's signature adven-
ture tours – the **Siberia
Experience** (☎03-443
4385; www.siberiaexperience.
co.nz; adult/child $355/287).
This thrill-seeking
extravaganza combines a
25-minute scenic small-
plane flight, a three-
hour tramp through the
remote mountain valley
and a half-hour jetboat
trip down the Wilkin and
Makarora Rivers. There
may be better ways to
spend four hours, but it's
tough to think of any.

This terrific valley can
also be reached on the
Gillespie Pass Circuit
(www.doc.govt.nz), a
magnificent 58km, three-
to four-day loop for ex-
perienced, well-equipped
hikers. The side trip to
Crucible Lake is one of
our favourite day tramps.

The Drive » Boom! Classic
Central Otago scenery – wide,
open, and framed by schist
peaks – welcomes you as SH6

snakes away from Makarora and sidles along the convoluted edges of Lake Wanaka and Lake Hawea. This glorious, 64km drive to Wanaka takes around an hour.

TRIP HIGHLIGHT

8 Wanaka (p101)

While certainly more laid-back than its amped-up sibling, Queenstown, Wanaka is not a sleepy hamlet any more. Its lakeside setting is utterly sublime, its streets less cluttered and clogged with traffic. Combine this with a critical mass of shops, restaurants and bars, and you've got an arguably more charming (and slightly cheaper) rival.

There's also an endless array of adrenalising and inspiring outdoor activities. Wanaka is the gateway to Mt Aspiring National Park, as well as Cardrona and Treble Cone ski resorts. Closer to town, however, are heaps of easier and more accessible adventures; see DOC's *Wanaka Outdoor Pursuits* pamphlet for a comprehensive run-down.

A classic walkway hoofs it up to the 527m summit of **Mt Iron** (1½ hours return), revealing panoramic views of Lake Wanaka and its mind-boggling surrounds. To get out on the lake, just jump right in wearing your underpants – or your swimsuit, obviously,

if you have one – or head out for a paddle with **Wanaka Kayaks** (☏0800 926 925; www.wanakakayaks. co.nz; Ardmore St; ◷9am-6pm Oct-Easter), located on the waterfront.

The Drive ›› Head over to Queenstown via the well-signposted Crown Range, NZ's highest sealed road at 1121m. Pull over at designated lookout points to admire the view on the way down to the Wakatipu Basin, and at the junction with SH6 head right towards Queenstown. This 68km drive will take just over an hour.

----

9 Queenstown (p96)

New Zealand's premier resort town is an extravaganza of shopping, dining and tour booking offices, packaged up together in the midst of inspiring mountain surrounds. If you're looking to let your hair down and tick some big stuff off your bucket list, Queenstown's a beaut place to do it.

Ease your way into it by walking around the town, taking in major sites such as **Skyline Gondola** and **Steamer Wharf**, and following **Queenstown Gardens'** lakeshore path, revealing ever-changing panoramas of Lake Wakatipu and the Remarkables. Add to this backdrop the region's other mountain ranges, tumbling rivers, hidden canyons and rolling high country, and

it's not hard to see why Queenstown is the king of outdoor adventure.

The options are mind-boggling, so allow us to suggest one of the classics – a blast on the **Shotover Jet** (☏03-442 8570; www.shotover jet. com; Gorge Rd, Arthurs Point; adult/child $135/75). Quite likely to be the most hair-raising boat ride of your life, this trip through a rocky canyon features famous 360-degree spins that may well blow your toupee clean off.

The Drive ›› This dramatic 60km drive through the Kawarau Gorge will take around an hour. Drive on SH6A out of Queenstown past the airport and then onwards beyond Lake Hayes and the turn-off for Arrowtown. There are numerous temptations on the way to Cromwell including Gibbston Valley wineries and the original AJ Hackett bungy jump.

----

10 Cromwell (p106)

The hot, dry, highly mineral soils around Cromwell account for the town's claim to fame as a fruit bowl – as celebrated in the giant, gaudy fruit sculpture that greets visitors as they arrive.

Among many luscious specimens are the grapes grown around **Bannockburn**, Central Otago's finest wine-growing subregion, just south of Cromwell. A dozen or so wineries are open to the public, with several offering notable dining.

Carrick (📞03-445 3480; www.carrick.co.nz; Cairnmuir Rd , Bannockburn; ⊙11am-5pm) is up there with the best, with an art-filled restaurant opening out on to a terrace and lush lawns, and a willow-framed view of the Carrick mountains. Their platters are a pleasurable complement to the wine range, which includes an intense, spicy pinot noir – their flagship drop – as well as a rich, toasty chardonnay and citrusy aromatic varietals.

Designated drivers can blow off some steam at the **Highlands Motor-sport Park** (📞03-445 4052; www.highlands.co.nz; cnr SH6 & Sandflat Rd; ⊙10am-5pm), a first-rate 4km racing circuit offering an array of high-octane experiences. Budding speed freaks can start out on the go-karts before taking a 200km/h ride in the Highlands Taxi, then completing three laps of the circuit as a passenger in a Porsche GT, or behind the wheel of a V8 muscle car.

The Drive ⟫ From Cromwell cross the bridge over Lake Dunstan and drive north on SH8 along the lake, through Tarras, and on to Lindis Pass before passing into Mackenzie Country. Around 9km after Twizel is the turn-off for Aoraki/Mt Cook on SH80. This 204km journey should take less than three hours.

- - - - - - - - - - - - - - -

⑪ Aoraki/Mt Cook National Park (p93)

The spectacular 700-sq-km Aoraki/Mt Cook National Park, along with Fiordland, Aspiring and Westland National Parks, forms part of the Te Wāhipounamu–South West New Zealand World Heritage Area, which extends from Westland's Cook River down to

DETOUR: MT ASPIRING NATIONAL PARK

Start: ⑧ Wanaka

Verdant valleys, alpine meadows, unspoiled rivers, craggy mountains and more than 100 glaciers make Mt Aspiring National Park an outdoor enthusiast's paradise. Protected as a national park in 1964, and now part of **Te Wāhipounamu–South West New Zealand World Heritage Area**, the park blankets 3555 sq km along the Southern Alps. Lording over it all is colossal Tititea/Mt Aspiring (3033m), the highest peak outside the Aoraki/Mt Cook area.

While the southern end of the national park near Glenorchy includes better-known tramps such as the Routeburn and Greenstone & Caples tracks, the Wanaka gateway offers an easier way in via Raspberry Creek, at the end of Mt Aspiring Rd, 50km from town – much of it along the lake shore. Well worth the drive in itself, even if you don't fancy tramping, the road is unsealed for 30km and involves nine ford crossings; it's usually fine in a 2WD, except in very wet conditions.

A good option for intermediate hikers, taking three to four hours return, **Rob Roy Glacier Track** is a chance to see glaciers, waterfalls and a swing bridge, among other landmarks. The **West Matukituki Valley Track**, meanwhile, heads up to historic Aspiring Hut, popular with overnight walkers. Sound tempting? Check out DOC's *Matukituki Valley Tracks* brochure (www.doc.govt.nz). Check in with **Tititea Mt Aspiring National Park Visitor Centre** (📞03-443 7660; www.doc.govt.nz; cnr Ardmore & Ballantyne Sts; ⊙8.30am-5pm daily Nov-Apr, Mon-Sat May-Oct) in Wanaka if the weather looks remotely dubious – even these lower-altitude tracks can be troublesome.

Fiordland. Fenced in by the Southern Alps and the Two Thumb, Liebig and Ben Ohau Ranges, more than one-third of the national park has a blanket of permanent snow and glacial ice.

The highest *maunga* (mountain) in the park is mighty **Aoraki/Mt Cook** – at 3754m it's the tallest peak in Australasia. Among the region's other many great peaks are Sefton, Tasman, Silberhorn, Malte Brun, La Perouse, Hicks, De la Beche, Douglas and the Minarets.

Unless you're an able alpinist, the best way to view this mountain majesty is on a scenic flight. **Helicopter Line** (☏03-435 1801; www.helicopter.co.nz; Glentanner Park, Mt Cook Rd) and **Mount Cook Ski**

Planes (☏03-430 8026; www.mtcookskiplanes.com; Mt Cook Airport) will buzz you around the peaks on a variety of trips; all but the shortest include a landing in the snow.

The Drive ›› Return along SH80, pausing at lookout points along the 55km stretch to soak up more of the mesmerising lake and mountain scenery. At the junction with SH8 turn left and drive a further 47km

Field of lupines overlooking Lake Tekapo

northeast over the Mary Range to Lake Tekapo.

TRIP HIGHLIGHT

⑫ Lake Tekapo (p91)

The mountain-ringed basin known as the Mackenzie Country – lined with surreal blue hydro lakes and canals, surrounded by golden tussock – is one of the South Island's most celebrated landscapes. Toward its northern boundary is Lake Tekapo township, born of a hydropower scheme completed in 1953, and today pretty much a compulsory stopping point for the passing traveller.

Perched on the shore of the opalescent, turquoise lake, with a backdrop of the snowcapped Southern Alps, it's no wonder the Church of the Good Shepherd is one of NZ's most photographed buildings. Built of stone and oak in 1935, it features a picture window that frames a distractingly divine view of lake and mountain majesty. Arrive early morning or late afternoon if you want to avoid the crowds.

The view is indeed divine, but still no match for the epic, 360-degree panorama from the top of **Mt John** (1029m). A winding but well-sealed road leads to the summit, home to astronomical observatories and fabulous Astro Café (p92). You can also reach the summit via the circuit track (2½ hours return).

The Drive » Climb away from the lake on SH8 over the relatively low Burkes Pass (709m) and on to the rural town of Fairlie, home of super-fine pies. From here, drive on SH79 through flatter but still rolling countryside to Geraldine, the cheese and pickle capital of New Zealand. Total distance is 89km.

- - - - - - - - - -

⑬ Geraldine (p91)

With a touch of quaint English village about it, Geraldine is a pleasant place to break a journey amid the rural Canterbury Plains.

On the town's north-western fringe, **Talbot Forest Scenic Reserve** (www.doc.govt.nz; Tripp St) is a good place to stretch your legs and hug some magnificent trees, including lofty kahikatea (white pine) and a massive totara estimated to be around 800 years old.

The forest lends its name to one of Geraldine's signature attractions, Talbot Forest Cheese (p91). You'll find it in the Four Peaks Plaza alongside Barker's, the pickle-makers that will complete your ploughman's lunch.

GETTING ON THE PISTE

The South Island is an essential southern-hemisphere destination for snow bunnies, with downhill skiing, cross-country (Nordic) skiing and snowboarding all passionately pursued. NZ's ski season is generally June through September, though it varies considerably from one resort to another, and can run as late as October.

NZ's ski fields come in all shapes and sizes. Some people like to be near Queenstown's party scene, others prefer the quality high-altitude runs on Mt Hutt or less-stressed and cheaper club-skiing areas. These are some of our favourite South Island skiing and snowboarding spots:

Treble Cone (☎03-443 1406, snow-phone 03-443 7444; www.treblecone.com; day lift pass adult/child $106/52) The highest and largest of the Southern Lakes ski areas is in a spectacular location 26km from Wanaka, with steep slopes suitable for intermediate to advanced skiers (and a rather professional vibe). There are also halfpipes and a terrain park for boarders.

Coronet Peak (☎03-442 4620; www.nzski.com; Coronet Peak Rd; day lift pass adult/child $104/59) At the Queenstown region's oldest ski field, snow-making and treeless slopes provide excellent skiing and snowboarding for all levels. There's night skiing Friday and Saturday.

Cardrona (☎03-443 8880, snow phone 03-443 7007; www.cardrona.com; Cardrona Skifield Access Rd; day lift pass adult/child $101/52; ◷9am-4pm Jul-Sep) Around 34km from Wanaka, with several high-capacity chairlifts, beginners tows and Parks 'n' Pipes for the freestylers.

Mt Hutt (☎03-302 8811; www.nzski.com; day lift pass adult/child $98/56; ◷9am-4pm) One of the highest ski areas in the southern hemisphere, located close to Methven. There are plenty of beginner, intermediate and advanced slopes.

Ohau (☎03-438 9885; www.ohau.co.nz; day lift pass adult/child $83/34) This commercial ski area is on Mt Sutton, 42km from Twizel. There are plenty of intermediate and advanced runs, excellent snowboarding, two terrain parks and Lake Ohau Lodge.

Snowboarding, Methven

The Drive » Drive north on SH72, crossing the braided Rangitata River after 6km, then passing through flat, irrigated pastoral land along Roman-straight roads. Continue on SH72 as it traces around the eastern edge of the mountains. Turn right on to SH77, 72km from Geraldine, and drive the last 10km to Methven.

⑭ Methven (p90)

Methven is busiest in winter, when it fills up with snow bunnies heading to nearby Mt Hutt ski field. At other times tumbleweeds don't quite blow down the main street – much to the disappointment of the wannabe gunslingers arriving for the raucous October rodeo. Over summer it's a low-key and affordable

base for explorations into the spectacular mountain foothills.

The town itself can be explored on a heritage trail and the **Methven Walk/Cycleway**. Maps for these are available from the **i-SITE** (☎03-302 8955; www.methvenmthutt. co.nz; 160 Main St; ⏰9.30am-5pm daily Jul-Sep, 9am-5pm Mon-Fri, 10am-3pm Sat & Sun Oct-Jun; 🛜), which can also provide information about other activities in the area including horse riding, hot-air balloon trips and jetboat trips on the nearby Rakaia Gorge.

The Drive » Drive north on Mt Hutt Station Rd and then turn right on to SH72, passing through Mt Hutt village before reaching the beautifully blue and braided river at Rakaia Gorge, 16km from Methven.

⑮ Rakaia Gorge

One of NZ's most voluminous braided rivers, the Rakaia starts out deep and swift in the mountains before gradually widening and separating into strands over a gravel bed. The half-day **Rakaia Gorge Walkway** is a good opportunity to survey the river's milky blue waters and take in other sites including the historic ferryman's cottage and old coal mines.

The Drive » Drive east on SH72 (aka Rte 77) for 41km to Darfield, leaving the mountains in the rear-view mirror as you reach the patchwork Canterbury Plains. Continue east on SH73, until the outskirts of Christchurch, then follow signs for the city centre. Total distance is 88km.

Milford Sound Majesty

4

Explore two totally different Southern Lakes resorts – thrilling Queenstown and tranquil Te Anau – before following New Zealand's premier wilderness highway to majestic Milford Sound.

TRIP HIGHLIGHTS

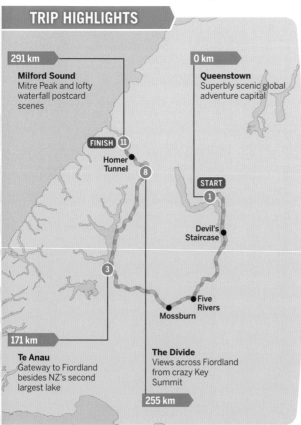

291 km

Milford Sound
Mitre Peak and lofty waterfall postcard scenes

FINISH 11
Homer Tunnel
8

0 km

Queenstown
Superbly scenic global adventure capital

START
1

Devil's Staircase

3

Five Rivers
Mossburn

171 km

Te Anau
Gateway to Fiordland besides NZ's second largest lake

The Divide
Views across Fiordland from crazy Key Summit

255 km

3–4 DAYS
291KM / 181 MILES

GREAT FOR...

BEST TIME TO GO

Summer and autumn; the Homer Tunnel is sometimes closed due to avalanche risk in winter and spring.

 ESSENTIAL PHOTO

Mitre Peak standing sentry above Milford Sound.

 BEST FOR WATERFALLS

Te Anau–Milford Hwy after a drop of rain or two.

Left Walking path, Milford Sound (p60)

4 Milford Sound Majesty

A well-beaten path this may well be, but its bookends are nothing short of sublime – Queenstown, buzzing with adrenaline and fuelled up on fabulous food and wine; and at the other end Milford Sound, New Zealand's most famous sight. In between is a series of eye-popping, often untouched wilderness landscapes, with the lovely lakeside town of Te Anau a handy base for exploring them.

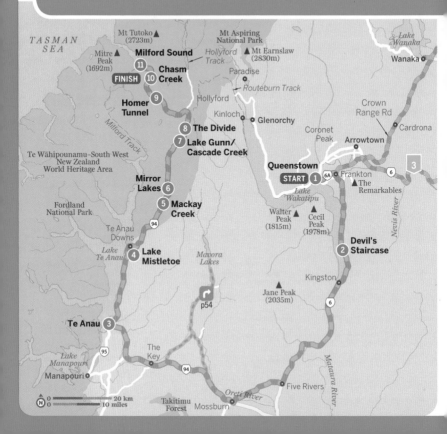

1 Queenstown (p96)

A small town with a big attitude, Queenstown is synonymous with the outdoors, and often crazy adventures such as bungy jumping, skydiving and jetboating. Then there's the other Queenstown – the one with the cosmopolitan restaurant and arts scene, excellent vineyards and five world-class golf courses. For the best of both worlds, it's hard to beat.

If that weren't enough, Queenstown goes for gold with an utterly sublime setting along the meandering shore of Lake Wakatipu, framed by the jagged peaks of the Remarkables. To soak up the town's scenery, stroll along Steamer Wharf to **Queenstown Gardens** (Park St), the leafy peninsula just five minutes' walk away. The

lakeside track affords ever-changing panoramas of the lake and surrounds, while its interior sports lush lawns, fine trees, rose gardens and occasional curiosities, including the fun and free **frisbee golf course** (www.queenstowndiscgolf.co.nz).

The Drive » Head east along SH6A to Frankton, then turn onto SH6 south signposted for Te Anau. Skirting past the Kelvin Peninsula at the foot of the Remarkables, the road then follows the eastern shore of Lake Wakatipu with stunning alpine views either side of the highway. The distance from Queenstown to the Devil's Staircase is 35km.

2 Devil's Staircase

The views along the shores of Lake Wakatipu, NZ's longest and third-largest lake, are distractingly beautiful, with the Remarkables and Hector ranges rising to the east, Cecil Peak and the Fyfe Mountains to the west, and the deep blue lake in between.

This is a winding drive ripe for rubbernecking, so keep your eyes on the road and your hands upon the wheel. Look out for the well-signposted Devil's Staircase, the aptly named lookout point that punctuates a tortuous section of road that winds up, over and around the lake edge. Pull over, jump out, breathe in that clear

mountain air and revel in the amazing views.

The Drive » Continue along SH6. The topography flattens as you approach Five Rivers, 58km from the Devil's Staircase. Turn right for Mossburn and the junction with SH94. Turn right and drive 60km northwest to Te Anau. At the Key, 34km from Mossburn, the Fiordland mountains appear for the first time. This 136km drive should take around two hours.

3 Te Anau (p113)

Peaceful, lakeside Te Anau township is the main gateway to Fiordland National Park and ever-popular Milford Sound, as well as a pleasant place to while away a few days. It's large enough to have a smattering of good eateries and places to stay, but it's much easier on the liver and wallet than attention-grabbing Queenstown.

The lake, NZ's second-largest, was gouged out by a huge glacier and has several arms that extend into the mountainous, forested western shore. Hidden away on this side, accessible only by boat, are the **Te Anau Glowworm Caves**, which first surfaced in Māori legend and were subsequently 'rediscovered' in 1948. The 200m-long cave system is a magical wonderland of strange rock forms, whirlpools and waterfalls. The

LINK YOUR TRIP

3 Southern Alps Circuit

From Queenstown, embark on this granddaddy of road trips taking in the best of the South Island's mountain scenery.

glittering pièce de résistance is the glow-worm grotto in its inner reaches. **Real Journeys** (www.realjourneys.co.nz; ☎0800 656 501; 85 Lakefront Dr; ⏰7.30am-8.30pm Sep-May, 8am-7pm Jun-Aug) runs 2¼-hour guided tours, reaching the heart of the caves via a lake cruise, walkway and a short underground boat ride.

The Drive » Follow the signs to one of NZ's most scenic drives – the Te Anau–Milford Hwy, which traces the lake edge for most of the way to the Lake Mistletoe car park (28km).

❹ Lake Mistletoe

It's an easy amble through manuka (tea tree) scrub and regenerating mountain beech forest to this compact and serene glacial lake. Beside the lake, an excellent place for a picnic, there are great views of the mountain ranges that make up some of the vast Fiordland National Park.

On the lake and among the surrounding rushes and flax you're likely to see resident scaup (ducks), and if you look really carefully you may spot native frogs hopping about.

The frogs (known to Māori as pepeketua) are of the genus *Leiopelma*, a primitive group of amphibians that have hardly changed over millions of years.

The Drive » Continue north on SH94 for around 1km before cutting inland at Te Anau Downs and heading up the Eglinton Valley. After another 21km you will reach Mackay Creek.

❺ Mackay Creek

One of many well-signposted spots to pull over and soak up the Milford Rd's majesty, Mackay Creek offers an

DETOUR:
MAVORA LAKES

Start: ❸ Te Anau

Mavora Lakes Conservation Park (www.doc.govt.nz; Centre Hill Rd), in the Snowdon State Forest, lies within the Te Wāhipounamu–South West New Zealand World Heritage Area. As the crow flies the park is relatively close to the tourist honeypots of Queenstown, Te Anau and the Milford Rd, but a slow, gravel road and spartan facilities (long-drop toilets, water supply and firepits) mean that only the eager venture in.

The heart of the park is the sublime Mavora Lakes camping area, huge golden meadows sitting alongside two lakes – North and South Mavora – fringed by forest and towered over by the impressive Thomson and Livingstone Mountains with peaks rising to more than 1600m. Cloaked in beech, the valley walls pitch steeply skyward, terminating in ranges of rocky peaks that contrast starkly against the undulating blanket of golden grassland on the valley floor.

If you're camping or in a campervan, this is a tranquil place to stay, although it can get busy during the school summer holidays (December to January).

Those short on time can still savour its serenity on a 2½-hour walk that circumnavigates the smaller South Mavora Lake. On the western edge of the lake the track passes through mature beech forest, while on the other side it traverses large grassy flats. There are two scenic, springy swing bridges to cross, views galore and squadrons of birds – from honking flocks of waterfowl in the marsh to tiny rifleman and robins flitting through the forest.

Reach Mavora Lakes via Centre Hill Rd, 14km west of Mossburn on SH94. From there, it's another 38km, heading north along a mostly unsealed road, to South Mavora Lake.

CRUISING THE SOUND

There's no getting around it: no visit to Fiordland is complete without a trip to Milford Sound (Piopiotahi), the first sight of which will likely knock your socks off (if the drive there hasn't already). Sheer rocky cliffs rise out of still, dark waters, and forests clinging to the slopes sometimes relinquish their hold, causing a 'tree avalanche' into the drink. The spectacular, photogenic 1692m-high **Mitre Peak/ Rahotu** rises dead ahead – its image has dominated NZ tourism brochures since year dot and is one of few vistas truly worthy of the word 'iconic'.

A postcard will never do it justice, and a big downpour will only add to the drama. The average annual rainfall of 7m is more than enough to fuel cascading waterfalls and add a shimmering moody mist to the scene, while the freshwater sitting atop warmer seawater replicates deep-ocean conditions, encouraging the activity of marine life such as dolphins, seals and penguins.

A cruise is Milford Sound's most accessible experience, as evident from the armada of companies berthed at the waterfront cruise terminal. Each company claims to be quieter, smaller, bigger, cheaper, or in some way preferable to the rest. What really makes a difference is the timing of the cruise. Most bus tours aim for 1pm sailings, so if you avoid that time of day there will be fewer people on the boat, fewer boats on the water and fewer buses on the road. With some companies you get a better price on cruises outside rush hour, too. If you're particularly keen on wildlife, ask whether there will be a nature guide on board.

escape from the sweet but somewhat claustrophobic confines of the beech forest to the open surrounds of the Eglinton Valley.

There's little here except for basic camping, picnic benches, and the wonderfully expansive views of the valley and vertiginous Earl Mountains, which provide a taste of what's to come. The creek is particularly photogenic in late spring when the lupins lining its banks are gloriously in bloom. Take care when pulling off or turning back on to the highway, as visibility is poor.

All the viewpoints and nature walks lining the Te Anau–Milford Hwy are detailed in DOC's *Fiordland National Park Day Walks* brochure, available online (www.doc.govt.nz) or from the Fiordland National Park Visitor Centre in Te Anau.

The Drive » Drive for 7km along the Eglinton River valley flats and through beech forest until you see the DOC sign for Mirror Lakes.

- - - - - - - - - - - -

❻ Mirror Lakes

The boardwalk at Mirror Lakes takes you through beech forest and wetlands, and on a calm day the lakes reflect the Earl Mountains across the valley and the harakeke (flax) that fringes the water. Head here early in the morning for your best chance of seeing double. If, however, your arrival coincides with a tour bus, be prepared for a swarm of snap-happy tourists as multitudinous as the sandflies.

The lakes area is also a good place to spot bird life, such as scaup, South Island kaka, ruru (morepork) and robins. Also keep an eye and ear out for the endangered mohua (yellowhead), with its colourful plumage and machine-gun-like chitter-chatter. In 2015 the valley's mohua population was bolstered by the relocation of 80 birds from a predator-free island sanctuary in Dusky Sounds, testament to the dedication of local conservationists.

The Drive » Continue driving north mainly through red beech forest, with occasional glimpses

WHY THIS IS A CLASSIC TRIP
LEE SLATER, WRITER

I must have seen Milford Sound and the Eglinton Valley in online articles and glossy magazines a thousand times, and visited on at least a dozen occasions. And yet I'm still blown away by its World Heritage grandeur. My ideal Milford Sound trip involves sunny, blue skies on the way there, followed by torrential rain fuelling the lofty waterfalls and raging rivers.

Top: Campsite at Mavora Lakes (p54)
Left: Mackay Falls on the Milford Track (p97)
Right: Entrance to Te Anau Glowworm Caves (p53)

of the valley and mountains. It's a 20-minute, 19km drive from Mirror Lakes to Lake Gunn.

- - - - - - - - - - - - -

⑦ Lake Gunn/ Cascade Creek

The area around Cascade Creek and Lake Gunn, known to Māori as O Ta-para, was a regular stop-over for parties heading to Anita Bay in search of *pounamu* (greenstone). The **Lake Gunn Nature Walk** (45 minutes return) loops through tall red beech forest ringing with birdsong, with side trails leading to peaceful lakeside beaches.

The Drive » From Lake Gunn/ Cascade Creek, continue driving north for 7km to the Divide. You'll pass the smaller Lake Fergus and Lake Lochie along the way.

- - - - - - - - - - - - -

TRIP HIGHLIGHT

⑧ The Divide

Stunted silver beech predominates as you make your way up to the harsher environs of the Divide, the lowest east–west pass in the Southern Alps. The car park and shelter here serve hikers on the Routeburn, and Greenstone & Caples Tracks, both of which head off from this point.

A marvellous two-hour return walk can be had along the start of the Routeburn, ascending (in gut-busting fashion) through beech forest to the alpine tussockland of **Key Summit**. The nature walk around the

boggy tops, festooned with mountain flax, snow totara and Dr Seuss–esque *dracophyllum,* is a great excuse to linger, while on a good day the 360-degree panorama encompasses the Hollyford, Eglinton and Greenstone Valleys, and Lake Marian basin with pyramidal Mt Christina (2474m). The view is truly worth the effort, but in anything less than clear weather, don't even go there.

The Drive >> From the Divide, SH94 snakes west, passing Marian Corner where safety gates will be closed if there is a risk of avalanche further along. The road then passes Camera Flat and climbs through the cascade-tastic upper Hollyford Valley to the Homer Tunnel. It's 16km from the Divide to the tunnel entrance.

- - - - - - - - - - - - - -

9 Homer Tunnel

Framed by a spectacular, high-walled, ice-carved amphitheatre, the 1270m-long Homer Tunnel is the only vehicular access point for Milford Sound.

Begun as a relief project in the 1930s' Depression and finally opened to motor traffic in 1954, the tunnel is one way, with inflows controlled by traffic lights. During the summer months, this can mean delays of up to 20 minutes while you wait for the lights to turn green, but when immersed in such a spectacular environment, who cares?

Dark, rough-hewn and dripping with water, the tunnel emerges at the other end at the head of the spectacular **Cleddau Valley**. Any spare 'wows' might pop out about now. Kea (alpine parrots) loiter in gangs around the tunnel entrance looking to mug tourists for scraps of food, but don't feed them as it's bad for their health.

The Drive >> From the parking area on the Milford Sound side of the Homer Tunnel to Chasm Creek it's a 9km drive. If it's wet or has been raining, waterfalls cascading down the Cleddau

FIORDLAND NATIONAL PARK

Fiordland National Park is arguably NZ's finest outdoor treasure. At 12,607 sq km it is the country's largest national park, making up half of the Te Wāhipounamu–South West New Zealand World Heritage Area, and one of the largest in the world. You don't have to look too hard to see why it buddies up with the Egyptian pyramids and the Grand Canyon on the World Heritage list.

It is jagged and mountainous, densely forested and cut through by numerous deeply recessed sounds (technically fiords) that reach inland like crooked fingers from the Tasman Sea. Indeed, one of the first impressions visitors gain of the park is of the almost overpowering steepness of the mountains, an impression accentuated by the fact that the mountains are usually separated only by narrow valleys. Formed during the glacial periods of the last ice age, its peaks are very hard and have eroded slowly, compared to the mountains of Mt Aspiring and Arthur's Pass, which are softer. Gentle topography this is not. It is raw and hard-core all the way.

High annual rainfall – delivered across the Tasman Sea – results in super-lush vegetation. Inland forests feature red, silver and mountain beech, while coastal forest is dominated by podocarp species such as matai, rimu and totara as well as the red-bloomed southern rata. Fiordland is well known to bird-watchers as the home of the endangered takahe, but more commonly spotted are kereru (NZ pigeons), riflemen, tomtits, fantails, bush robins, tui, bellbirds and kaka, as well as kea and rock wrens in alpine areas. If you wander around at night you might occasionally hear a kiwi.

It's around 85 million years since the snippet of land that became NZ split off from Gondwanaland; Fiordland makes it seem like just yesterday.

Right Routeburn Track (p97)

Valley walls resemble brooding skies streaked with bolts of lightning.

PICHUGIN DMITRY/SHUTTERSTOCK ©

⑩ Chasm Creek

The **Chasm Creek Walk** is an easy 20-minute return walk from the car park and well worth a stop come rain or shine. The forest-cloaked Cleddau River plunges through scooped-out boulders in a narrow chasm, creating deep falls and a natural rock bridge. The power of the surging waters is awe-inspiring and more than a little frightening. A quick dip is definitely off the cards. Along the way, look out for glimpses of Mt Tutoko (2723m), Fiordland's highest peak, above the beech forest.

The Drive » The final 10km to Milford Sound continues down the Cleddau Valley, passing the Tutoko River suspension bridge at around the halfway point.

TRIP HIGHLIGHT

⑪ Milford Sound (p116)

Sydney Opera House, Big Ben, the Eiffel Tower – Milford Sound is up there with the best of them, which explains why it receives about half a million visitors each year, many of them crammed into the peak months (January and February). Some 14,000 arrive on foot via the Milford Track, which ends at the Sound. Many more drive from Te Anau,

TOP TIP:
MILFORD MAYHEM

To evade Milford's crowds, leave Te Anau early (by 8am) or later in the morning (11am) to avoid the tour buses heading for midday cruises. Be sure to fill up with petrol in Te Anau, and note that chains must be carried on icy or avalanche-risk days from May to November.

but most arrive via the multitude of bus tours. But don't worry: out on the water all this humanity seems tiny compared to nature's vastness.

Milford Sound

And getting out on the water is a must. Fortunately there are cruises galore, but kayak trips offer an even more mind-blowing perspective of this monumental landscape. Te Anau–based **Rosco's Milford Kayaks** (📞03-249 8500, 0800 476 726; www.roscos milfordkayaks.com; 72 Town Centre; trips $99-199; ⊙Nov-Apr) offers guided, tandem kayak trips including the 'Morning Glory' ($199), a challenging paddle the full length of the fiord to Anita Bay, and the less strenuous 'Stirling Sunriser' ($195), which ventures beneath the 151m-high **Stirling Falls**.

Although Milford Sound is best appreciated from the water or air, killer views of Mitre Peak can still be enjoyed on the 30-minute interpretive **Foreshore Walk**.

Destinations

Marlborough & Nelson (p64)

Explore this fertile region to find sunshine, water, wine and whales.

Christchurch & Canterbury (p81)

An inspirational go-getting city leads to looming peaks in the Southern Alps.

Queenstown & Wanaka (p96)

Hit this adrenaline-addled destination for adventures, stunning scenery and world-class wine.

The West Coast (p108)

Powerful glaciers grind towards wild, windswept coasts.

Fiordland & Southland (p113)

This scenic wonderland thrills with majestic mountains, mighty fiords and turquoise lakes.

Snowboarding, Queenstown (p96)
KYLE SPARKS/GETTY IMAGES ©

These top-of-the-South neighbours have much in common beyond an amenable climate: both boast renowned coastal holiday spots, particularly the Marlborough Sounds, Abel Tasman National Park and Kaikoura.

Marlborough & Nelson

Picton

◉ Sights

Edwin Fox Maritime Museum MUSEUM
(www.edwinfoxsociety.co.nz; Dunbar Wharf; adult/child $15/5; ⊘9am-5pm) Purportedly the world's ninth-oldest surviving wooden ship, the *Edwin Fox* was built near Calcutta and launched in 1853. During its chequered career it carried troops to the Crimean War, convicts to Australia and immigrants to NZ. This museum has maritime exhibits, including the venerable old dear herself.

Picton Museum MUSEUM
(London Quay; adult/child $5/1; ⊘10am-4pm) If you dig local history – whaling, sailing and the 1964 Roller Skating Champs – this will float your boat. The photo displays are well worth a look, especially for five bucks.

Activities

Nine Dives DIVING
(☑0800 934 837, 03-573 7199; www.ninedives.co.nz; trips $195-350) Offers dive trips around the Sounds taking in marine reserves and various wrecks including the *Mikhail Lermontov*, plus diver training. Snorkelling seal-swims also available ($150).

☞ Tours

Marlborough Tour Company TOUR
(☑0800 990 800, 03-577 9997; www.marlboroughtourcompany.co.nz; Town Wharf; adult/child $145/59; ⊘departs 1.30pm) Runs the 3½-hour 'Seafood Odyssea' cruise to a salmon farm, complete with an ocean bounty and sauvignon blanc tasting.

Sleeping

★Jugglers Rest HOSTEL $
(☑03-573 5570; www.jugglersrest.com; 8 Canterbury St; sites from $20, dm $33, d $75-85; ⊘closed Jun-Sep; @🛜) 🚲 Jocular hosts keep all their balls in the air at this well-run, ecofriendly, bunk-free backpackers. Peacefully located a 10-minute walk from town, or even less on a free bike. Cheery gardens are a good place to socialise with fellow travellers, especially during the occasional circus-skills shows.

Buccaneer Lodge LODGE $
(☑03-573 5002; www.buccaneerlodge.co.nz; 314 Waikawa Rd, Waikawa; s $90, d $99-124; 🛜) This Waikawa Bay lodge offers tidy, basic en suite rooms, many with expansive views of the Sounds from the 1st-floor balcony. Town transfers, bike hire and home-baked bread come courtesy of the kindly owners.

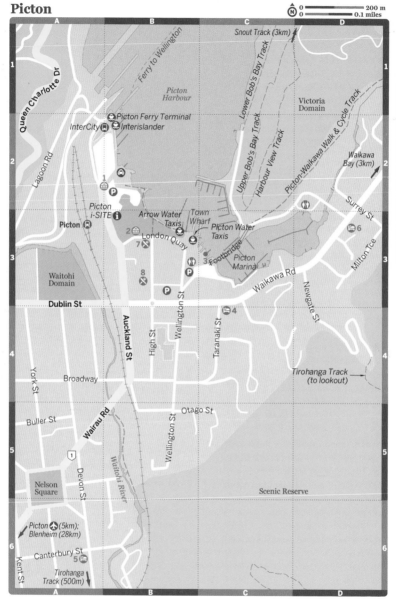

Picton Top 10 Holiday Park HOLIDAY PARK **$**
(☏ 0800 277 444, 03-573 7212; www.pictontop10.
co.nz; 70 Waikawa Rd; sites from $36, units $75-185;
@ 🛜 🏊) About 500m from town, this com-
pact, well-kept park has plenty of lawn and
picnic benches, plus crowd-pleasing facilities including a playground, barbecue area
and swimming pool.

Picton

⊙ Sights
1 Edwin Fox Maritime Museum..............B2
2 Picton Museum B3

⊕ Activities, Courses & Tours
3 Marlborough Tour Company..............C3

⊜ Sleeping
4 Harbour View Motel............................C4
5 Jugglers Rest...A6
6 Picton Top 10 Holiday Park.................D3

⊗ Eating
7 Café Cortado B3
8 Gusto B3

★ **Whatamonga Homestay**   HOMESTAY **$$**

(☑ 03-573 7192; www.whsl.co.nz; 425 Port Underwood Rd; d incl breakfast $180; @🕾) Follow Waikawa Rd, which becomes Port Underwood Rd, for 8km and you'll bump into this classy waterside option – two self-contained units with king-sized beds and balconies with magic views. Two other rooms under the main house share a bathroom. Free kayaks, dinghies and fishing gear are available. Minimum two-night stay.

Harbour View Motel   MOTEL **$$**

(☑ 03-573 6259, 0800 101 133; www.harbourviewpicton.co.nz; 30 Waikawa Rd; d $145-185; 🕾) Its elevated position means this motel com-

mands good views of Picton's mast-filled harbour from its smart, self-contained studios with timber decks.

Eating

Gusto   CAFE **$**

(33 High St; meals $11-21; ⊙ 7.30am-2.30pm) This friendly and hard-working joint does beaut breakfasts including first-class salmon-scrambled eggs and a 'Morning Glory' fry-up worth the calories. Lunch options may include local mussels or a steak sandwich.

Picton Village Bakkerij   BAKERY **$**

(cnr Auckland & Dublin Sts; bakery items $2-8; ⊙ 6am-4pm Mon-Fri, to 3.30pm Sat; ✍) Dutch owners bake trays of European goodies here, including interesting breads, filled rolls, cakes and custardy, tarty treats. An excellent stop before or after the ferry, or to stock a packed lunch.

Café Cortado   CAFE **$$**

(www.cortado.co.nz; cnr High St & London Quay; mains $16-34; ⊙ 8am-late) A pleasant corner cafe and bar with sneaky views of the harbour through the foreshore's pohutukawa and palms. This consistent performer turns out fish dishes, homemade cheeseburgers and decent pizza.

ⓘ Information

Picton i-SITE (☑ 03-520 3113; www.marlboroughnz.com; Foreshore; ⊙ 8am-5pm Mon-Fri, to 4pm Sat & Sun) All vital tourist guff including maps, Queen Charlotte Track information, lockers and transport bookings. Dedicated Department of Conservation (DOC) counter.

Havelock

Sights

If a stroll through the streets of Havelock leaves you thinking that there *must* be more to this area, you're right – and to get a taste of it you need go no further than the **Cullen Point Lookout**, a 10-minute drive from Havelock along Queen Charlotte Dr. A short walk leads up and around a headland overlooking Havelock, the surrounding valleys and Pelorus Sound.

Information on local sights and activities can be found at the Havelock i-SITE, which shares its home with the Eyes On Nature museum, chock-full of frighteningly lifelike,

full-size replicas of birds, fish and other critters.

And of course, there is plenty to see and do when you are exploring the Marlborough Sounds themselves.

🏃 Activities

Pelorus Eco Adventures
KAYAKING
(☑0800 252 663, 03-574 2212; www.kayak-newzealand.com; Blue Moon Lodge, 48 Main Rd; per person $175) Float in an inflatable kayak on scenic Pelorus River, star of the barrel scene in *The Hobbit*. Wend your way down exhilarating rapids, through crystal-clear pools and past native forest and waterfalls. No experience required. Minimum two people.

Nydia Track
TRAMPING
(www.doc.govt.nz) The Nydia Track (27km, 10 hours) starts at Kaiuma Bay and ends at Duncan Bay (or vice versa). You'll need water and road transport to complete the journey; Havelock's Blue Moon Lodge runs a shuttle to Duncan Bay.

🛌 Sleeping

★Hopewell
LODGE $
(☑03-573 4341; www.hopewell.co.nz; 7204 Kenepuru Rd, Double Bay; dm/cottages from $40/195, d with/without bathroom from $140/105; @🛜) Beloved of travellers from near and far, remote Hopewell sits waterside surrounded by native bush. Savour the long, winding drive to get there, or take a water taxi from Te Mahia ($20). Stay at least a couple of days, so you can chill out or enjoy the roll-call of activities: mountain biking, kayaking, sailing, fishing, eating gourmet pizza, soaking in the outdoor hot tub, and more.

Blue Moon Lodge
HOSTEL $
(☑03-574 2212, 0800 252 663; www.bluemoonhavelock.co.nz; 48 Main Rd; dm $33, r with/without bathroom from $96/82; @🛜) 🍃 This pleasant and relaxed lodge has homely rooms in the main house, a spa family unit ($160), and cabins and a bunkhouse in the yard. Notable features include a sunny barbecue deck, inflatable kayak trips on the Pelorus River, and Nydia Track transport.

Havelock Garden Motels
MOTEL $$
(☑03-574 2387; www.gardenmotels.com; 71 Main Rd; d $125-160; 🛜) Set in a large, graceful garden complete with dear old trees and blooms galore, these 1960s units have been tastefully revamped to offer homely

comforts. Local activities are happily booked for you.

ℹ Information

Havelock i-SITE (☑03-577 8080; www.pelorusnz.co.nz; 61 Main Rd; ⊙9am-5pm summer only) Helpful wee visitor centre.

Blenheim

◉ Sights

★Omaka Aviation Heritage Centre
MUSEUM
See p26

Pollard Park
PARK
(Parker St) Ten minutes' walk from town, this 25-hectare park boasts beautiful blooming and scented gardens, a playground, tennis courts, croquet and a nine-hole golf course. It's pretty as a picture when lit up on summer evenings. Five minutes away, on the way to or from town, is the extensive **Taylor River Reserve**, a lovely place for a stroll.

Marlborough Museum
MUSEUM
(☑03-578 1712; www.marlboroughmuseum.org.nz; 26 Arthur Baker Pl, off New Renwick Rd; adult/child $10/5; ⊙10am-4pm) Besides a replica street-scene, vintage mechanicals and well-presented historical displays, there's the *Wine Exhibition*, for those looking to cap off their vineyard experiences.

Taylor River Reserve, Blenheim
DAVID WALL PHOTO/GETTY IMAGES ©

Marlborough Wine Region

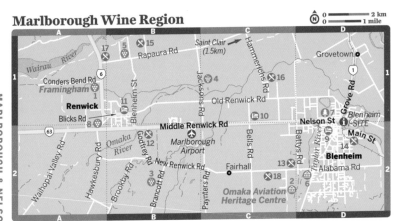

Marlborough Wine Region

◎ Top Sights
1 Framingham A1
2 Omaka Aviation Heritage
   Centre C2

◎ Sights
3 Brancott Estate Heritage
   Centre B2
4 Cloudy Bay C1
5 Huia B1
6 Marlborough Museum D2
7 Pollard Park D1
8 Te Whare Ra A1

◎ Sleeping
9 Lugano Motorlodge D2
10 St Leonards C1
11 Watson's Way Lodge B1

◎ Eating
12 Arbour B2
13 Burleigh C2
14 Gramado's D2
15 Herzog Winery B1
16 Rock Ferry C1
17 Wairau River Restaurant A1
18 Wither Hills C2

🏃 Activities

★ Driftwood Eco-Tours KAYAKING, ECOTOUR
(☑03-577 7651; www.driftwoodecotours.co.nz; 749
Dillons Point Rd; kayak tours $70-180, 4WD tours for
2/3 people from $440/550) Go on a kayak or
4WD tour with passionate locals Will and
Rose for fascinating tours on and around
the ecologically and historically significant
Wairau Lagoon, just 10 minutes' drive from
Blenheim. Rare birds and the muppety
Royal Spoonbill may well be spotted. The
self-contained 'retreat' offers accommodation for up to four people (double/quad
$190/310; breakfast extra $15 per person)
next to the Opawa River.

Wither Hills Farm Park WALKING
In a town as flat as a pancake, this hilly
11-sq-km park provides welcome relief, offering over 60km of walking and mountain-
biking trails with grand views across the
Wairau Valley and out to Cloudy Bay. Pick up
a map from the i-SITE or check the information panels at the many entrances including
Redwood St and Taylor Pass Rd.

☞ Tours

Highlight Wine Tours TOUR
(☑03-577 9046, 027 434 6451; www.highlightwine
tours.co.nz) Visit a chocolate factory, too.
Custom tours available.

Bubbly Grape Wine Tours TOUR
(☑027 672 2195, 0800 228 2253; www.bubbly
grape.co.nz) Three different tours including a
gourmet lunch option.

Sounds Connection TOUR
(☑03-573 8843, 0800 742 866; www.sounds
connection.co.nz) This operator partners up
with **Herzog Winery** (☑03-572 8770; www.
herzog.co.nz; 81 Jefferies Rd; mains $24-36; ⊙12-
3pm & 6-9pm Wed-Sun) for a wine-and-food-
matched lunch.

Bike2Wine TOUR
(☑ 03-572 8458, 0800 653 262; www.bike2wine.
co.nz; 9 Wilson St, Renwick; standard/tandem per
day $30/60, pick ups from $10) An alternative
to the usual minibus tours – get around the
grapes on two wheels. This operator offers
self-guided, fully geared and supported
tours.

🛏 Sleeping

Blenheim Top 10
Holiday Park HOLIDAY PARK $
(☑ 03-578 3667, 0800 268 666; www.blenheim
top10.co.nz; 78 Grove Rd; sites $45, cabins $80-92,
units & motel $135-145; @ 🛜 ⛱) Ten minutes'
walk to town, this holiday park spreads out
under and alongside the main road bridge
over the Opawa River. Ask for the quietest
spot available. Cabins and units are tidy
but plain-Jane, set in a sea of asphalt. Fun-
time diversions include a spa, a pool, a playground and bike hire.

Watson's Way Lodge LODGE $
(☑ 03-572 8228; www.watsonswaylodge.com; 56
High St, Renwick; campervans per person $18, d &
tw $98; ⊙ closed Aug-Sep; @ 🛜) This traveller-
focused lodge has spick-and-span en suite
rooms in a sweetly converted bungalow with
a full kitchen and comfy lounge. There are
also spacious leafy gardens dotted with fruit
trees and hammocks, an outdoor claw-foot
bath, bikes for hire (guest/public rate $18/28
per day) and local information aplenty.

171 on High MOTEL $$
(☑ 0800 587 856, 03-579 5098; www.171on
highmotel.co.nz; 171 High St; d $145-185; 🛜) A
welcoming option close to town, these taste-
ful, splash-o-colour studios and apartments
are bright and breezy in the daytime, warm
and shimmery in the evening. Expect a wide
complement of facilities and 'extra mile'
service.

Lugano Motorlodge MOTEL $$
(☑ 03-577 8808, 0800 584 266; www.lugano.co.nz;
91 High St; d $140-155; 🛜) In a prime location
opposite pretty Seymour Sq and a two-
minute walk to the centre of town, this is a
beige but smart and upmarket motel complex with modern conveniences. Ask about
the end unit with two balconies, or at least
plump for upstairs. Hush glass mutes the
main-road traffic noise.

★ St Leonards COTTAGES $$
(☑ 03-577 8328; www.stleonards.co.nz; 18 St Leon-
ards Rd; d incl breakfast $125-320; 🛜 ⛱) Tucked
into the 2-hectare grounds of an 1886 home-
stead, these five stylish and rustic cottages
offer privacy and a reason to stay put. Each
is unique in its layout and perspective on the
gardens and vines. Our pick is the capacious
and cosy Woolshed, exuding agricultur-
al chic. Resident sheep, chickens and deer
await your attention.

🍴 Eating & Drinking

★ Burleigh DELI $
(☑ 03-579 2531; 72 New Renwick Rd, Burleigh; pies
$6; ⊙ 7.30am-3pm Mon-Fri, 9am-1pm Sat) The
humble pie rises to stratospheric heights
at this fabulous deli; try the sweet pork-
belly or savoury steak and blue cheese, or
perhaps both. Fresh-filled baguettes, local
sausage, French cheeses and great coffee
also make tempting appearances. Avoid the
lunchtime rush.

Gramado's BRAZILIAN $$
(☑ 03-579 1192; www.gramadosrestaurant.com; 74
Main St; mains $26-38; ⊙ 4pm-late Tue-Sat) In-
jecting a little Latin American flair into the
Blenheim dining scene, Gramado's is a fun
place to tuck into unashamedly hearty meals
such as lamb *assado*, feijoada (smoky pork
and bean stew) and Brazilian-spiced fish.
Kick things off with a caipirinha, of course.

Dodson Street CRAFT BEER
(☑ 03-577 8348; www.dodsonstreet.co.nz; 1 Dodson St, Mayfield; ⊙ 11am-11pm) Pub and garden with a beer-hall ambience and suitably
Teutonic menu (mains $17 to $27) featuring
pork knuckle, bratwurst and schnitzel. The
stars of the show are the 24 taps pouring
quality, ever-changing craft beer, including award-winning brewer and neighbour,
Renaissance.

ℹ Information

Blenheim i-SITE (☑ 03-577 8080; www.
marlboroughnz.com; 8 Sinclair St, Blenheim
Railway Station; ⊙ 9am-5pm Mon-Fri, 9am-
3pm Sat, 10am-3pm Sun) Information on
Marlborough and beyond. Wine-trail maps and
bookings for everything under the sun.

Post Office (cnr Scott & Main Sts)

Wairau Hospital (☑ 03-520 9999; www.
nmdhb.govt.nz; Hospital Rd)

MARLBOROUGH WINERIES

Around 35 wineries are open to the public. Our picks of the bunch provide a range of high-quality cellar-door experiences, with most being open from around 10.30am till 4.30pm (some scale back operations in winter). Wineries may charge a small fee for tasting, normally refunded if you purchase a bottle. Pick up a copy of the *Marlborough Wine Trail* map from the Blenheim i-SITE (p69), also available online at www.wine-marlborough. co.nz. If your time is limited, pop into **Wino's** (www.winos.co.nz; 49 Grove Rd; ☉10am-7pm Sun-Thu, to 8pm Fri & Sat) in Blenheim, a sterling one-stop shop for some of Marlborough's finer and less common drops.

A Taste of the Tastings

Auntsfield Estate (☑03-578 0622; www.auntsfield.co.nz; 270 Paynters Rd, Blenheim; ☉11am-4.30pm Mon-Fri summer only)

Bladen (www.bladen.co.nz; 83 Conders Bend Rd, Renwick; ☉11am-4.30pm)

Brancott Estate Heritage Centre (www.brancottestate.com; 180 Brancott Rd, Blenheim; ☉10am-4.30pm)

Clos Henri Vineyard (www.clos-henri.com; 639 State Hwy 63, RD1, Blenheim; ☉10am-4pm Mon-Fri summer only)

Cloudy Bay (www.cloudybay.co.nz; 230 Jacksons Rd, Blenheim; ☉10am-4pm) 🍃

Forrest (www.forrest.co.nz; 19 Blicks Rd, Renwick; ☉10am-4.30pm)

Framingham (www.framingham.co.nz; 19 Conders Bend Rd, Renwick; ☉10.30am-4.30pm) 🍃

Huia (www.huia.net.nz; 22 Boyces Rd, Blenheim; ☉10am–5pm Oct-May) 🍃

Saint Clair Estate (www.saintclair.co.nz; 13 Selmes Rd, Rapaura; ☉9am-5pm)

Spy Valley Wines (www.spyvalleywine.co.nz; 37 Lake Timara Rd, Waihopai Valley; ☉10.30am-4.30pm daily summer, 10.30am-4.30pm Mon-Fri winter) 🍃

Kaikoura

👁 Sights

Point Kean Seal Colony　　WILDLIFE RESERVE

At the end of the peninsula seals laze around in the grass and on the rocks, lapping up all the attention. Give them a wide berth (10m), and never get between them and the sea – they will attack if they feel cornered and can move surprisingly fast.

Kaikoura Museum　　MUSEUM

(www.kaikoura.govt.nz; 14 Ludstone Rd; adult/child $5/1; ☉10am-4.30pm Mon-Fri, 2-4pm Sat & Sun) This provincial museum displays historical photographs, Māori and colonial artefacts, a huge sperm-whale jaw and the fossilised remains of a plesiosaur.

Fyffe House　　HISTORIC BUILDING

(www.heritage.org.nz; 62 Avoca St; adult/child $10/ free; ☉10am-5pm daily Oct-Apr, to 4pm Thu-Mon May-Sep) Kaikoura's oldest surviving building, Fyffe House has whale-bone founda-

tions that were laid in 1844. Proudly positioned and fronted with a colourful garden, the little two-storey cottage offers a fascinating insight into the lives of colonial settlers. Interpretive displays are complemented by historical objects, while peeling wallpaper and the odd cobweb lend authenticity. Cute maritime-themed shop.

🏃 Activities

★Kaikoura Peninsula Walkway　　WALKING

A foray along this walkway is a must-do. Starting from the town, the three- to four-hour loop heads out to Point Kean, along the cliffs to South Bay, then back to town over the isthmus (or in reverse, of course). En route you'll see fur seals and red-billed seagull and shearwater colonies. Lookouts and interesting interpretive panels abound. Collect a map at the i-SITE or follow your nose.

Kaikoura Coast Track　　TRAMPING

(☑03-319 2715; www.kaikouratrack.co.nz; 356 Conway Flat Rd, Ngaroma; per person $190) This easy two-day, 26km, self-guided walk across

Te Whare Ra (www.twrwines.co.nz; 56 Anglesea St, Renwick; ⊙11am-4.30pm Mon-Fri, noon-4pm Sat & Sun Nov-Mar) 🍷

Vines Village (www.thevinesvillage.co.nz; 193 Rapaura Rd, Rapaura; ⊙10am-5pm)

Wairau River (www.wairauriverwines.com; 11 Rapaura Rd, Blenheim; ⊙10am-5pm) 🍷

Yealands Estate (☑03-575 7618; www.yealandsestate.co.nz; cnr Seaview & Reserve Rds, Seddon; ⊙10am-4.30pm) 🍷

Wining & Dining

Arbour (☑03-572 7989; www.arbour.co.nz; 36 Godfrey Rd, Renwick; mains $31-38; ⊙3pm-late Tue-Sat year-round, 6pm-late Mon Jan-Mar; 🍷) Located in the thick of Renwick wine country, this elegant restaurant offers 'a taste of Marlborough' by focusing on local produce fashioned into contemporary yet crowd-pleasing dishes. Settle in for a three-, four- or multiple-course à la carte offering ($73/85/98), or an end-of-the-day nibble and glass or two from the mesmerising wine list.

Wairau River Restaurant (☑03-572 9800; www.wairauriverwines.com; cnr Rapaura Rd & SH6, Renwick; mains $21-27; ⊙noon-3pm) Modishly modified mud-brick bistro with wide veranda and beautiful gardens with plenty of shade. Order the mussel chowder, or the double-baked blue-cheese soufflé. Relaxing and thoroughly enjoyable.

Rock Ferry (☑03-579 6431; www.rockferry.co.nz; 80 Hammerichs Rd, Blenheim; mains $23-27; ⊙11.30am-3pm) Pleasant environment inside and out, with a slightly groovy edge. The compact summery menu – think roasted salmon and peppers or organic open steak sandwich – is accompanied by wines from Marlborough and Otago.

Wither Hills (☑03-520 8284; www.witherhills.co.nz; 211 New Renwick Rd, Blenheim; mains $24-33, platters $38-68; ⊙11am-4pm) Simple, well-executed food in a stylish space. Pull up a beanbag on the Hockneyesque lawns and enjoy smoked lamb, Asian pork belly or a platter, before climbing the ziggurat for impressive views across the Wairau.

private farmland combines coastal and alpine views. The price includes two nights' farm-cottage accommodation and pack transport; BYO sleeping bag and food. Starts 45km south of Kaikoura.

Clarence River Rafting RAFTING
(☑03-319 6993; www.clarenceriverrafting.co.nz; 1/3802 SH1, at Clarence Bridge; half-day trips adult/child $120/80) Raft the bouncy Grade II rapids of the scenic Clarence River on a half-day trip (2½ hours on the water), or on longer journeys including a five-day adventure with wilderness camping (adult/child $1400/900). Based on SH1, 40km north of Kaikoura near Clarence Bridge.

👉 Tours

Whale Watch Kaikoura ECOTOUR
See p34

Dolphin Encounter ECOTOUR
(☑03-319 6777, 0800 733 365; www.encounter-kaikoura.co.nz; 96 Esplanade; adult/child swim $175/160, observation $95/50; ⊙tours 8.30am & 12.30pm year-round, plus 5.30am Nov-Apr) 🐬 Claiming NZ's highest success rate (90%) for both locating and swimming with dolphins, this operator runs feel-good three-hour tours, which often encounter sizeable pods of sociable duskies – the classic Kaikoura treat.

Seal Swim Kaikoura ECOTOUR
(☑0800 732 579, 03-319 6182; www.sealswimkaikoura.co.nz; 58 West End; tours $70-110, viewing adult/child $55/35; ⊙Oct-May) Take a (warmly wet-suited) swim with Kaikoura's healthy population of playful seals – including very cute pups – on two-hour guided snorkelling tours (by boat) run by the Chambers family.

⭐ Albatross Encounter BIRDWATCHING
(☑0800 733 365, 03-319 6777; www.encounterkaikoura.co.nz; 96 Esplanade; adult/child $125/60; ⊙tours 9am & 1pm year-round, plus 6am Nov-Apr) 🐦 Even if you don't consider yourself a bird

Kaikoura

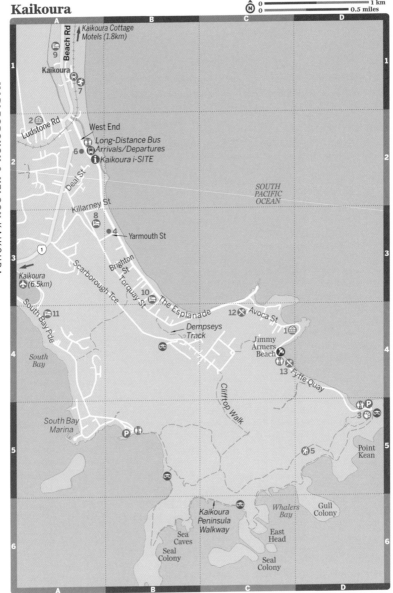

nerd, you'll love this close encounter with pelagic species such as shearwaters, shags, mollymawks and petrels. It's the various albatross species, however, that steal the show. Just awesome.

🛏 Sleeping

Albatross Backpacker Inn HOSTEL **$**
(📱 0800 222 247, 03-319 6090; www.albatross-kaikoura.co.nz; 1 Torquay St; dm $29-32, tw/d $69/74; 🕸) 🕭 This arty backpackers resides

Kaikoura

◎ Sights
1 Fyffe House	C4
2 Kaikoura Museum	A2
3 Point Kean Seal Colony	D5

✪ Activities, Courses & Tours
Albatross Encounter	(see 4)
4 Dolphin Encounter	B3
5 Kaikoura Peninsula Walkway	D5
6 Seal Swim Kaikoura	A2
7 Whale Watch Kaikoura	A1

🛏 Sleeping
8 Albatross Backpacker Inn	A3
9 Alpine Pacific Holiday Park	A1
10 Anchor Inn Motel	B3
11 Bay Cottages	A4

✖ Eating
Cafe Encounter	(see 4)
12 Green Dolphin	C4
13 Kaikoura Seafood BBQ	C4
Reserve Hutt	(see 6)

in three sweet buildings, one a former post office. It's colourful and close to the beach but sheltered from the breeze. As well as a laid-back lounge with musical instruments for jamming, there are decks and verandas to chill out on.

Alpine Pacific Holiday Park　HOLIDAY PARK $
(☑0800 692 322, 03-319 6275; www.alpine-pacific.co.nz; 69 Beach Rd; sites from $46, cabins $78, units & motels $137-200; @🕸🏊) This compact and proudly trimmed park copes well with its many visitors and offers excellent facilities, including a pool, hot tubs and a barbecue pavilion. Rows of cabins and units are a tad more stylish than the average, and mountain views can be enjoyed from many angles.

★Kaikoura Cottage Motels　MOTEL $$
(☑0800 526 882, 03-319 5599; www.kaikoura cottagemotels.co.nz; cnr Old Beach & Mill Rds; d $140-160; 🕸) This enclave of eight modern tourist flats looks mighty fine, surrounded by attractive native plantings. Oriented for mountain views, spick-n-span self-contained units sleep four between an open plan studio-style living room and one private bedroom. Proud, lovely hosts seal the deal.

Bay Cottages　MOTEL $$
(☑03-319 5506; www.baycottages.co.nz; 29 South Bay Pde; cottages/motel r $120/140; 🕸) Here's a great-value option on South Bay, a few kilometres south of town: five tourist cottages with kitchenette and bathroom that sleep up to four, and two slick motel rooms with stainless-steel benches, a warm feel and clean lines. The cheery owner may even take you crayfishing in good weather.

Anchor Inn Motel　MOTEL $$$
(☑03-319 5426; www.anchorinn.co.nz; 208 Esplanade; d $185-255; 🕸) The Aussie owners liked this Kaikoura motel so much they bought it and moved here. The sharp and spacious units are a pleasant 15-minute walk from town and about 10 seconds from the ocean.

✖ Eating

Reserve Hutt　CAFE $
(72 West End; meals $10-20; ⊗8.30am-3pm; ✐) The best coffee in town, roasted on-site and espressoed by cheery baristas in Kaikoura's grooviest cafe. Puttin' out that rootsy retro-Kiwiana vibe we love so much, this is a neat place to linger over a couple of flatties and down a chocolate brownie, delicious ham croissant or the full eggy brunch.

Cafe Encounter　CAFE $
(96 Esplanade; meals $8-23; ⊗7am-5pm; 🕸✐) This cafe in the Encounter Kaikoura complex is more than just somewhere to wait for your tour. The cabinet houses respectable sandwiches, pastries and cakes, plus there's a tasteful range of daily specials such as homemade soup and pulled-pork rolls. A sunny patio provides sea views.

Kaikoura Seafood BBQ　SEAFOOD $
(Fyffe Quay; items from $5; ⊗10.30am-6pm) Conveniently located on the way to the Point Kean seal colony, this long-standing roadside barbecue is a great spot to sample local seafood, including crayfish (half/full from $25/50) and scallops, at an affordable price.

★Green Dolphin　MODERN NZ $$$
(☑03-319 6666; www.greendolphinkaikoura.com; 12 Avoca St; mains $26-39; ⊗5pm-late) Kaikoura's consistent top-ender dishes up high-quality local produce including seafood, beef, lamb and venison, as well as seasonal flavours such as fresh tomato soup. There are lovely homemade pasta dishes, too. The hefty drinks list demands attention,

featuring exciting aperitifs, craft beer, interesting wines and more. Booking ahead is advisable, especially if you want to secure a table by the window and watch the daylight fade.

ℹ️ Information

Kaikoura i-SITE (☑ 03-319 5641; www.kaikoura.co.nz; West End; ⊙ 9am-5pm Mon-Fri, to 4pm Sat & Sun, extended hours Dec-Mar) Helpful staff make tour, accommodation and transport bookings, and help with DOC-related matters.

Nelson

👁️ Sights

⭐ **Tahuna Beach**   BEACH
Nelson's primo playground takes the form of an epic sandy beach (with lifeguards in summer) backed by dunes, and a large grassy parkland with a playground, an espresso cart, a hydroslide, bumper boats, a roller-skating rink, a model railway, and an adjacent restaurant strip. Weekends can get veerrrrry busy!

Suter Art Gallery   GALLERY
(www.thesuter.org.nz; 208 Bridge St; ⊙ 9.30am-4.30pm) **FREE** Adjacent to Queen's Gardens, Nelson's public art gallery presents changing exhibitions, floor talks, musical and theatrical performances, and films. The Suter's long-awaited reopening after a fabulous redevelopment is scheduled for late 2016. Check the website to confirm it's open, and to find out what's on.

Nelson Provincial Museum   MUSEUM
(☑ 03-548 9588; www.nelsonmuseum.co.nz; cnr Trafalgar & Hardy Sts; adult/child $5/3; ⊙ 10am-5pm Mon-Fri, to 4.30pm Sat & Sun) This modern museum space is filled with cultural heritage and natural history exhibits which have a regional bias, as well as regular touring exhibitions (for which admission fees vary). It also features a great rooftop garden.

Christ Church Cathedral   CHURCH
(www.nelsoncathedral.org; Trafalgar Sq; ⊙ 9am-6pm) **FREE** The enduring symbol of Nelson, the art-deco Christ Church Cathedral lords it over the city from the top of Trafalgar St. The best time to visit is during the 10am and 7pm Sunday services when you can hear the organist and the choir in song.

🏃 Activities

Gentle Cycling Company   BICYCLE TOUR
(☑ 0800 932 453, 03-929 5652; www.gentlecycling.co.nz; day tours $95-105) Self-guided cycle tours along the Great Taste Trail, with drop-ins (and tastings) at wineries, breweries, cafes and occasional galleries. Bike hire ($45 per day) and shuttles also available.

Trail Journeys   BICYCLE TOUR
(☑ 0800 292 538, 03-540 3095; www.trailjourneysnelson.co.nz; MD Outdoors, 1/37 Halifax St; full-day tours from $89) Trail Journeys offers a range of self-guided cycle tours around Nelson city, and beyond along the Great Taste Trail, based at three conveniently located depots in central Nelson, Mapua Wharf and Kaiteriteri.

Nelson Paragliding   PARAGLIDING
(☑ 03-544 1182; www.nelsonparagliding.co.nz) Get high in the sky over Tahunanui with Nelson Paragliding.

Kite Surf Nelson   KITESURFING
(☑ 0800 548 363; www.kitesurfnelson.co.nz) Learn to kitesurf at Tahunanui, or hire a stand-up paddle board.

👉 Tours

Nelson Tours & Travel   TOUR
(☑ 027 237 5007, 0800 222 373; www.nelsontoursandtravel.co.nz) CJ and crew run various small-group, flexible tours honing in on Nelson's wine, craft beer, art and scenic highlights. The five-hour 'Best of Both Worlds' combines indulgence with your special interest, be it galleries or a trip to Rabbit Island ($105). Day tours of Marlborough wineries also available ($195).

🛏️ Sleeping

Tahuna Beach
Kiwi Holiday Park   HOLIDAY PARK $
(☑ 03-548 5159, 0800 500 501; www.tahunabeachholidaypark.co.nz; 70 Beach Rd, Tahunanui; sites/cabins/units from $20/65/120; @ 🛜) Close to Tahuna Beach, 5km from Nelson, this mammoth park is home to thousands in high summer, which you'll either find hellish or bloody brilliant, depending on your mood. Off season, you'll have the cafe and minigolf mostly to yourself.

YHA Nelson by Accents   HOSTEL $
(☑ 03-545 9988, 0800 888 335; www.accentshostel.nz; 59 Rutherford St; dm/s $30/69, d with/without bathroom $119/89; @ 🛜) A tidy, well-

Central Nelson

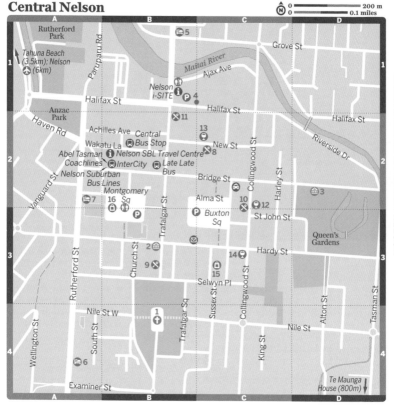

Central Nelson

◎ Sights
1 Christ Church Cathedral.......................B4
2 Nelson Provincial
   Museum..B3
3 Suter Art Gallery...............................D2

⊕ Activities, Courses & Tours
4 Trail Journeys...................................B1

⊟ Sleeping
5 Cedar Grove Motor
   Lodge..B1
6 Palazzo Motor Lodge.........................A4
7 YHA Nelson by Accents......................A2

⊗ Eating
8 DeVille...C2
9 Hopgood's......................................B3
10 Indian Café....................................C2
11 Stefano's.......................................B2

⊕ Drinking & Nightlife
12 Free House.....................................C2
13 Rhythm and Brown...........................C2
14 Sprig & Fern...................................C3

⊟ Shopping
15 Nelson Farmers' Market.....................C3
16 Nelson Market.................................B2

run, central hostel with spacious communal areas including well-equipped kitchens, a sunny terrace, a TV room and bike storage. Great local knowledge for tours and activities from new managers injecting

some personality into this YHA-affiliated establishment.

Palazzo Motor Lodge   MOTEL **$$**
(☏03-545 8171, 0800 472 5293; www.palazzo motorlodge.co.nz; 159 Rutherford St; studios

Cycling above Nelson
DAVID CHADWICK/GETTY IMAGES ©

$130-249, apt $230-390; 🗗) This modern, Italian-tinged motor lodge offers stylish studios and one- and two-room apartments featuring enviable kitchens with decent cooking equipment, classy glassware and a dishwasher. Its comfort and convenient location easily atone for the odd bit of dubious art.

Te Maunga House   B&B **$$**
(🗐 03-548 8605; www.nelsoncityaccommodation.co.nz; 15 Dorothy Annie Way; s $90, d $125-145; ⊘closed May-Oct; 🗗) Aptly named ('the mountain'), this grand old family home has exceptional views and a well-travelled host. Two doubles and a twin have a homely feel with comfy beds and their own bathrooms. Your hearty breakfast can be walked off up and down *that* hill, a 10-minute climb with an extra five minutes to town.

Cedar Grove Motor Lodge   MOTEL **$$**
(🗐 03-545 1133; www.cedargrove.co.nz; cnr Trafalgar & Grove Sts; d $155-210; 🗗) A big old cedar landmark, this smart, modern block of spacious apartments is just a three-minute walk to town. Its range of studios and doubles are plush and elegant, with full cooking facilities.

✗ Eating

Stefano's   PIZZA **$**
(🗐 03-546 7530; www.pizzeria.co.nz; 91 Trafalgar St; pizzas $6-29; ⊘noon-2pm & 4.30-9pm; 🖋) Located upstairs in the State Cinema complex, this Italian-run joint turns out the town's best pizza. Thin, crispy, authentic and delicious, with some variations a veritable bargain. Wash it down with a beer and chase it with a creamy dessert.

★DeVille   CAFE **$$**
(🗐 03-545 6911; www.devillecafe.co.nz; 22 New St; meals $12-21; ⊘8am-4pm Mon-Sat, 8.30am-2.30pm Sun; 🖋) Most of DeVille's tables lie in its sweet walled courtyard, a hidden boho oasis in the inner city and the perfect place for a meal or morning tea. The food's good and local – from fresh baking to a chorizo-burrito brunch, Caesar salad and proper burgers, washed down with regional wines and beers. Open late for live music Fridays in summer.

Indian Café   INDIAN **$$**
(🗐 03-548 4089; www.theindiancafe.com; 94 Collingwood St; mains $13-23; ⊘noon-2pm Mon-Fri, 5pm-late daily; 🖋) This saffron-coloured Edwardian villa houses an Indian restaurant that keeps the bhajis raised with impressive interpretations of Anglo-Indian standards such as chicken tandoori, rogan josh and beef madras. Share the mixed platter to start, then mop up your mains with one of 10 different breads.

★Hopgood's   MODERN NZ **$$$**
(🗐 03-545 7191; www.hopgoods.co.nz; 284 Trafalgar St; mains $27-40; ⊘5.30pm-late Mon-Sat) Tongue-and-groove-lined Hopgood's is perfect for a romantic dinner or holiday treat. The food is decadent and skilfully prepared but unfussy, allowing quality local ingredients to shine. Try confit duck with sour cherries, or pork belly and pine-nut butter. Desirable, predominantly Kiwi wine list. Bookings advisable.

☗ Drinking & Nightlife

★Free House   CRAFT BEER
(🗐 03-548 9391; www.freehouse.co.nz; 95 Collingwood St; ⊘3pm-late Mon-Fri, noon-late Sat, 10.30am-late Sun) Come rejoice at this church of ales. Tastefully converted from its original, more reverent purpose, it's now home to an excellent, oft-changing selection of NZ craft beers. You can imbibe inside, out, or even in a yurt, where there's regular entertainment. Hallelujah.

Rhythm and Brown   BAR
(🗐 03-546 56319; www.facebook.com/rhythmandbrown; 19 New St; ⊘4pm-late Tue-Sat) Nelson's

slinkiest late-night drinking den, where classy cocktails, fine wines and craft beer flow from behind the bar and sweet vinyl tunes drift from the speakers. Regular Saturday-night micro-gigs in a compact, groovy space.

Sprig & Fern CRAFT BEER
(📋 03-548 1154; www.sprigandfern.co.nz; 280 Hardy St; ⊙11am-late) This outpost of Richmond's Sprig & Fern brewery offers 18 brews on tap, from lager through to doppelbock and berry cider. No pokies, no TV, just decent beer, occasional live music and a pleasant outdoor area. Pizzas can be ordered in. Look for a second Sprig at 143 Milton St, handy to Founders Park.

🛍 Shopping

Nelson Farmers' Market MARKET
(📋 022 010 2776; www.nelsonfarmersmarket.org.nz; Morrison Sq, cnr Morrison & Hardy Sts; ⊙11am-4pm Wed) Weekly market full to bursting with local produce to fill your picnic hamper.

Nelson Market MARKET
(📋 03-546 6454; www.nelsonmarket.co.nz; Montgomery Sq; ⊙8am-1pm Sat) Don't miss Nelson Market, a big, busy weekly market featuring fresh produce, food stalls, fashion, local arts, crafts and buskers.

ℹ Information

After Hours & Duty Doctors (📋 03-546 8881; 96 Waimea Rd; ⊙8am-10pm)
Nelson Hospital (📋 03-546 1800; www.nmdhb.govt.nz; Waimea Rd)
Nelson i-SITE (📋 03-548 2304; www.nelsonnz.com; cnr Trafalgar & Halifax Sts; ⊙8.30am-5pm Mon-Fri, 9am-4pm Sat & Sun) A slick centre complete with DOC information desk for the low-down on national parks and walks (including Abel Tasman and Heaphy tracks). Pick up a copy of the *Nelson Tasman Visitor Guide*.
Post Office (www.nzpost.co.nz; 209 Hardy St)

Moutere Hills

The inland **Moutere Highway** to Motueka (signposted at Appleby on SH60) is a pleasant drive through gentle countryside dotted with farms, orchards and lifestyle blocks. Visitor attractions are fewer and further between, but it's a scenic drive, especially during high summer when roadside stalls are laden with fresh produce. The main set-

tlement along the way is **Upper Moutere**. Originally named Sarau by the German immigrants who first settled in the area, today it's a sleepy hamlet with a couple of notable stops. Look for the *Moutere Artisans* trail guide (www.moutereartisans.co.nz).

◉ Sights

Golden Bear Brewing Company BREWERY
(www.goldenbearbrewing.com; Mapua Wharf, Mapua) In Mapua village it won't be hard to sniff out the Golden Bear – a microbrewery with tons of stainless steel out back, and a dozen or so brews out front. Authentic Mexican food (burritos, quesadillas and huevos rancheros; meals $10 to $16) will stop you from getting a sore head, and there's regular live music on Friday nights and Sunday afternoons.

★ Waimea Estate WINERY
See p21

Höglund Art Glass GALLERY
(📋 03-544 6500; www.hoglundartglass.com; 52 Lansdowne Rd, Appleby; ⊙10am-5pm) Ola, Marie and their associates work the furnace to produce internationally acclaimed glass art. The process is amazing to watch, and the results beautiful to view in the gallery. The jewellery and penguins make memorable souvenirs if the signature vases are too heavy to take home.

🍴 Eating & Drinking

★ Jester House CAFE $
(📋 03-526 6742; www.jesterhouse.co.nz; 320 Aporo Rd, Tasman; meals $15-22; ⊙9am-5pm) Long-standing Jester House is reason alone to take this coastal detour, as much for its tame eels as for the peaceful sculpture gardens that encourage you to linger over lunch. A short, simple menu puts a few twists into staples (venison burger, lavender shortbread), and there is local beer and wines. It's 8km to Mapua or Motueka.

Jellyfish MODERN NZ $$
(📋 03-540 2028; www.jellyfishmapua.co.nz; Mapua Wharf, Mapua; lunch $16-24, dinner $24-34; ⊙9am-late; 🅿) Between the waterside location, sunny patio and inspired East–West menu you've got an A-grade all-day cafe. Local fish and other produce feature heavily as do fine wines and craft beer.

Moutere Inn `PUB`
See p23

Motueka

◉ Sights

Hop Federation `BREWERY`
(☑ 03-528 0486; www.hopfederation.co.nz; 483 Main Rd, Riwaka; ⊙ 11am-6pm) Pop in for tastings ($3) and fill a flagon to go at this teeny-weeny but terrific craft brewery 5km from Mot. Our pick of the ales is the Red IPA. (And note the cherry stall across the road.)

Motueka District Museum `MUSEUM`
(☑ 03-528 7660; www.motuekadistrictmuseum. org.nz; 140 High St; admission by donation; ⊙ 10am-4pm Mon-Fri Dec-Mar, to 3pm Tue-Fri Apr-Nov) Interesting collection of regional artefacts, housed in a dear old school building.

✦ Activities

★ **Skydive Abel Tasman** `ADVENTURE SPORTS`
(☑ 03-528 4091, 0800 422 899; www.skydive. co.nz; Motueka Aerodrome, 60 College St; jumps 13,000/16,500ft $299/399) Move over, Taupo: we've jumped both and think Mot takes the cake. Presumably so do the many sports jumpers who favour this drop zone, some of whom you may see rocketing in. Photo and

Motueka

video packages are extra. Excellent spectating from the front lawn.

Tasman Sky Adventures `SCENIC FLIGHTS`
(☑ 0800 114 386, 027 223 3513; www.skyadventures.co.nz; Motueka Aerodrome, 60 College St; 15/30min flights $105/205) A rare opportunity to fly in a microlight. Keep your eyes open and blow your mind on a scenic flight above Abel Tasman National Park. Wow. And there's tandem hang gliding for the brave (15/30 minutes, 2500/5280ft $195/330).

⛏ Sleeping

★ **Motueka Top 10**
Holiday Park `HOLIDAY PARK $`
(☑ 03-528 7189; www.motuekatop10.co.nz; 10 Fearon St; sites from $48, cabins $69-160, units & motels $113-457; @ 🛜 ⊠) ✎ Close to town and the Great Taste Trail, this place is packed with grassy, green charm – check out those lofty kahikatea trees! Shipshape communal amenities include a swimming pool, spa and jumping pillow, and there are ample accommodation options from smart new cabins to an apartment sleeping up to 11. On-site bike hire, plus local advice and bookings freely offered.

Eden's Edge Lodge `HOSTEL $`
(☑ 03-528 4242; www.edensedge.co.nz; 137 Lodder Lane, Riwaka; sites from $18, dm $31, d/tr with bathroom $99/86; 🛜) ✎ Surrounded by farmland, 4km from the bustle of Motueka, this purpose-built lodge comes pretty close to backpacker heaven. Well-designed facilities include a gleaming kitchen and inviting communal areas including a grassy garden. There's bike hire for tackling the Great Taste Trail, but it's also within walking distance of beer, ice cream and coffee.

★ **Equestrian Lodge Motel** `MOTEL $$`
(☑ 0800 668 782, 03-528 9369; www.equestrian lodge.co.nz; Avalon Ct; d $125-158, q $175-215; 🛜 ⊠) No horses, no lodge, but no matter. This excellent motel complex is close to town (off Tudor St) and features expansive lawns, rose gardens, and a heated pool and spa alongside a series of continually refreshed units. Cheerful owners will hook you up with local activities.

Resurgence `LODGE $$$`
(☑ 03-528 4664; www.resurgence.co.nz; 574 Riwaka Valley Rd; d lodge from $695, chalets from $575; @ 🛜 ⊠) ✎ Choose a luxurious

en suite lodge room or a self-contained chalet at this magical green retreat. It's located a 15-minute drive from Abel Tasman National Park, and a 30-minute walk from the picturesque source of the Riwaka River. Lodge rates include aperitifs and a four-course dinner as well as breakfast; chalet rates are for B&B, with dinner an extra $120.

✕ Eating

Patisserie Royale   BAKERY $

(152 High St; baked goods $2-8; ⊙ 5am-5pm Mon-Fri, to 3pm Sat & Sun; 🖉) The best of several Mot bakeries and worth every delectable calorie. Lots of French fancies, delicious pies and bread with bite.

★ Toad Hall   CAFE $$

(🖉 03-528 6456; www.toadhallmotueka.co.nz; 502 High St; breakfast $10-20, lunch $10-23; ⊙ 8am-6pm, to 9pm summer) This fantastic cafe serves smashing breakfasts, such as smoked salmon rösti, and wholesome yet decadent lunches including pork-belly burgers. The sweet outdoor space is home to live music and pizza on Friday and Saturday nights in summer.

🍷 Drinking & Nightlife

Sprig & Fern   CRAFT BEER

(🖉 03-528 4684; www.sprigandfern.co.nz; Wallace St; ⊙ 2pm-late) A member of the local Sprig & Fern brewery family, this back-street tavern is the pick of Motueka's drinking holes. Small and pleasant, with two courtyards, it offers 20 hand-pulled brews, simple food (pizza, platters and an awesome burger; meals $15 to $23) and occasional live music.

☆ Entertainment

Gecko Theatre   CINEMA

(🖉 03-528 9996; www.geckotheatre.co.nz; 23b Wallace St; tickets $9-13) Pull up an easy chair at this wee, independent theatre and see interesting art-house flicks.

ℹ Information

Motueka i-SITE (🖉 03-528 6543; www.motuekaisite.co.nz; 20 Wallace St; ⊙ 8.30am-5pm Mon-Fri, 9am-4pm Sat & Sun) An endlessly busy info centre with helpful staff handling bookings from Kaitaia to Bluff and providing local national-park expertise and necessaries.

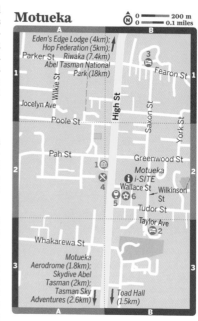

Motueka

◎ Sights
1 Motueka District Museum A2

🛏 Sleeping
2 Equestrian Lodge Motel.......................B3
3 Motueka Top 10 Holiday Park............ B1

✕ Eating
4 Patisserie Royale A2

🍷 Drinking & Nightlife
5 Sprig & Fern..................................B2

☆ Entertainment
6 Gecko Theatre...............................B2

Nelson Lakes National Park

🏃 Activities

There are two fantastic day hikes to be had. The five-hour **Mt Robert Circuit Track** starts at Mt Robert car park – a short drive from St Arnaud, serviced by **Nelson Lakes Shuttles** (🖉 027 547 6896, 03-547 6896; www.nelsonlakesshuttles.co.nz) – and circumnavigates the mountain. The optional side trip

Lake Rotoiti, Nelson Lakes National Park

along Robert Ridge offers staggering views into the heart of the national park. Alternatively, the **St Arnaud Range Track** (five hours return), on the east side of the lake, climbs steadily to the ridgeline adjacent to Parachute Rocks.

Rainbow   SKIING, SNOWBOARDING
(☑03-521 1861, snow phone 0832 226 05; www.skirainbow.co.nz; day lift pass adult/child $75/35) The sunny Nelson region has a ski area, just 100km away (a similar distance from Blenheim). Rainbow borders the Nelson Lakes National Park, with varied terrain, minimal crowds and good cross-country skiing. Chains are often required. St Arnaud is the closest town (32km).

🛏 Sleeping

Kerr Bay DOC Campsite   CAMPGROUND $
(www.doc.govt.nz; unpowered/powered sites per person $10/15) Near the Lake Rotoiti shore, the hugely popular Kerr Bay campsite has powered sites, toilets, hot showers, a laundry and a kitchen shelter. It's an inspiring base for your adventures, but do book in advance. Overflow camping is available around at DOC's **West Bay Campsite** (☑03-521 1806; sites $6; ☉summer), which is more basic.

★**Alpine Lodge**   LODGE $$
(☑03-521 1869; www.alpinelodge.co.nz; Main Rd, St Arnaud; d $155-210; @☎) Family owned and a consistent performer, this large lodge complex offers a range of accommodation, the pick of which are the split-level doubles with mezzanine bedroom and spa. If nothing else, go for the inviting in-house restaurant – a snug affair sporting an open fire, mountain views, good food (meals $10 to $32; takeaway pizza $20) and local beer.

Nelson Lakes Motels   MOTEL $$
(☑03-521 1887; www.nelsonlakes.co.nz; Main Rd, St Arnaud; d $125-140, q $135-180; ☎) These log cabins and newer board-and-batten units offer all the creature comforts, including kitchenettes and Sky TV. Bigger units have full kitchens and sleep up to six.

ℹ Information

DOC Nelson Lakes Visitor Centre (☑03-521 1806; www.doc.govt.nz; View Rd; ☉8am-4.30pm, to 5pm in summer) The Nelson Lakes Visitor Centre proffers park-wide information (weather, activities) and hut passes, plus displays on park ecology and history.

Christchurch & Canterbury

After visiting dynamic and inspiring Christchurch, explore Canterbury's Southern Alps, with Aoraki/ Mt Cook, the country's tallest peak, standing sentinel over this diverse region.

Christchurch

Welcome to a vibrant city in transition, coping creatively with the aftermath of NZ's second-worst natural disaster. Traditionally the most English of NZ cities, Christchurch's heritage heart was all but hollowed out following the 2010 and 2011 earthquakes that left 186 people dead.

Today Christchurch boasts more road cones and repurposed shipping containers than anywhere else in the world, waypoints in an epic rebuild that sees construction sites throughout the CBD. There is dust, noise, and heavy traffic at times. But don't be deterred. The city centre is graced by numerous notable arts institutions, the stunning Botanic Gardens and Hagley Park. Inner-city streets conceal art projects and pocket gardens, dotted among a thinned-out cityscape featuring remnant stone buildings and the sharp, shiny architecture of the new.

Curious travellers will revel in this chaotic, crazy and colourful mix, full of surprises and inspiring in ways you can't even imagine. And despite all the hard work and heartache, the locals will be only too pleased to see you.

◎ Sights

★**Christchurch Botanic Gardens** GARDENS
(www.ccc.govt.nz; Rolleston Ave; ⊙7am-8.30pm Oct-Mar, to 6.30pm Apr-Sep) Strolling through these blissful 30 riverside hectares of arboreal and floral splendour is a consummate Christchurch experience. Gorgeous at any time of the year, the gardens are particularly impressive in spring when the rhododendrons, azaleas and daffodil woodland are in riotous bloom. There are thematic gardens to explore, lawns to sprawl on, and a playground adjacent to the **Botanic Gardens Information Centre** (☑03-941 8999; ⊙9am-4pm Mon-Fri, 10.15am-4pm Sat & Sun).

★**Christchurch Art Gallery** GALLERY
(☑03-941 7300; www.christchurchartgallery.org. nz; cnr Montreal St & Worcester Blvd; ⊙10am-5pm Thu-Tue, to 9pm Wed) **FREE** Damaged in the earthquakes, Christchurch's fantastic art gallery has reopened brighter and bolder, presenting a stimulating mix of primarily NZ exhibitions.

Hagley Park PARK
(Riccarton Ave) Wrapping itself around the Botanic Gardens, Hagley Park is Christchurch's biggest green space, stretching for 165 hectares. Riccarton Ave splits it in two and the Avon River snakes through the north half.

It's a great place to stroll, whether on a foggy autumn morning, or a warm spring day when the cherry trees lining Harper Ave are in flower. Joggers make the most of the tree-lined avenues, year-round.

Canterbury Museum
MUSEUM

(☑ 03-366 5000; www.canterburymuseum.com; Rolleston Ave; ⊙ 9am-5pm) FREE Yes, there's a mummy and dinosaur bones, but the highlights of this museum are more local and more recent. The Māori galleries contain some beautiful *pounamu* (greenstone) pieces, while Christchurch Street is an atmospheric walk through the colonial past. The reproduction of Fred & Myrtle's gloriously kitsch Paua Shell House embraces Kiwiana at its best, and kids will enjoy the interactive displays in the Discovery Centre (admission $2). Hour-long guided tours commence at 3.30pm on Tuesday and Thursday.

Quake City
MUSEUM

(www.quakecity.co.nz; 99 Cashel St; adult/child $20/free; ⊙ 10am-5pm) A must-visit for anyone interested in the Canterbury earthquakes and conveniently located in the Re:START Mall, this compact museum tells stories through photography, video footage and various artefacts, including bits that have fallen off the cathedral. Most affecting of all is the film featuring locals recounting their own experiences.

Transitional Cathedral
CHURCH

(www.cardboardcathedral.org.nz; 234 Hereford St; entry by donation; ⊙ 9am-5pm, to 7pm summer)

Universally known as the Cardboard Cathedral due to the 98 cardboard tubes used in its construction, this interesting structure serves as both the city's temporary Anglican cathedral and as a concert venue. Designed by Japanese 'disaster architect' Shigeru Ban, the entire building was up in 11 months.

Arts Centre
HISTORIC BUILDING

(www.artscentre.org.nz; 2 Worcester Blvd) Dating from 1877, this enclave of Gothic Revival buildings was originally Canterbury College, the forerunner of Canterbury University. The college's most famous alumnus was the father of nuclear physics Lord Ernest Rutherford, the NZ physicist who first split the atom in 1917 (that's him on the $100 bill).

You'll have to be content to admire the architecture from the street, as the complex was badly damaged in the earthquakes. Some parts were due to reopen during 2016, with the whole project due for completion in 2019.

Cathedral Square
SQUARE

Christchurch's city square stands largely flattened and forlorn amid the surrounding rebuild, with the remains of ChristChurch Cathedral emblematic of the loss. The February 2011 earthquake brought down the 63m-high spire, while subsequent earthquakes in June 2011 and December 2011 destroyed the prized stained-glass rose window. Other heritage buildings around the square were also badly damaged, but one modern landmark left unscathed is the 18m-high metal sculpture *Chalice*, designed by Neil Dawson. It was erected in 2001 to commemorate the new millennium.

🏃 Activities

Antigua Boat Sheds
BOATING, KAYAKING

(☑ 03-366 6768; www.boatsheds.co.nz; 2 Cambridge Tce; ⊙ 9am-5pm) Dating from 1882, the photogenic green-and-white Antigua Boat Sheds hires out rowing boats ($35), kayaks ($12), Canadian canoes ($35) and bikes (adult/child $10/5); all prices are per hour. There's also a good cafe.

City Cycle Hire
BICYCLE RENTAL

(☑ 03-377 5952; www.cyclehire-tours.co.nz; bike hire half-/full day from $25/35) Offers door-to-door delivery of on- and off-road city bikes and touring bikes. Will also meet you with a bike at the top of the gondola if you fancy a 16km descent ($70 including gondola ride; 1½ hours).

👉 Tours

⭐ Tram
TRAM

(📱 03-377 4790; www.tram.co.nz; adult/child $20/
free; ⊙ 9am-6pm Oct-Mar, 10am-5pm Apr-Sep)
Excellent driver commentary makes this so
much more than a tram ride. The beautifully
restored old dears trundle around a 17-stop
loop, leaving every 15 minutes, taking in a
host of city highlights including Cathedral
Sq and New Regent St. The full circuit takes
just under an hour, and you can hop-on and
hop-off all day.

Christchurch Free Tours
WALKING TOUR

(www.freetours.co.nz; Cathedral Sq; ⊙ 11am) **FREE**
Yes, a free tour. Just turn up at the *Chalice*
sculpture in Cathedral Sq and look for the
red-T-shirted person. If you enjoy your two-
hour amble, tip your guide. Nice!

Christchurch Bike
& Walking Tours
CYCLING, WALKING

(📱 0800 733 257; www.chchbiketours.co.nz; 2
Cambridge Tce) See the city's highlights on an
informative, two-hour bicycle tour (adult/
child $50/30) or two-hour walking tour
(adult/child $35/20). Tours leave from the
Antigua Boat Sheds at 10am and 2pm daily;
bookings are essential.

🛏 Sleeping

Amber Kiwi Holiday Park
HOLIDAY PARK $

(📱 03-348 3327, 0800 348 308; www.amberpark.
co.nz; 308 Blenheim Rd, Riccarton; sites $42-50,
units $82-200; @🛜) Blooming lovely gardens
and close proximity to the city centre make
this urban holiday park a great option for
campervaners and tenters. Tidy cabins and
more-spacious motel units are also available.

Pomeroy's on Kilmore
B&B $$

(📱 03-374 3532; www.pomeroysonkilmore.co.nz;
282 Kilmore St; r $145-195; P🛜) Even if this
cute wooden house wasn't the sister and
neighbour of Christchurch's best craft-beer
pub, it would still be one of our favourites.
Three of the five elegantly furnished, en suite
rooms open on to a sunny garden. Rates in-
clude breakfast at Little Pom's (p87) cafe.

Focus Motel
MOTEL $$

(📱 03-943 0800; www.focusmotel.com; 344 Dur-
ham St N; r $160-250; P🛜) Sleek and central-
ly located, this friendly motel offers studio
and one-bedroom units with big-screen TVs,
iPod docks, kitchenettes and super-modern
decor. There's a guest barbecue and laundry,
and pillow-top chocolates sweeten the deal.

Transitional Cathedral
LINDA MCKIE /GETTY IMAGES ©

CentrePoint on Colombo
MOTEL $$

(📱 03-377 0859; www.centrepointoncolombo.
co.nz; 859 Colombo St; r/apt from $165/195; P🛜)
The friendly Kiwi-Japanese management
has imbued this centrally located motel with
style and comfort. Little extras such as stere-
os, blackout curtains and spa baths (in the
deluxe rooms) take it to the next level.

Lorenzo Motor Inn
MOTEL $$

(📱 03-348 8074; www.lorenzomotorlodge.co.nz;
36 Riccarton Rd; units $169-239; P🛜) There's a
Mediterranean vibe to this trim two-storey
motel – the best of many on the busy Riccarton Rd strip. Units range from studio to
two-bedroom apartments; some have spa
baths and little balconies.

⭐ George
HOTEL $$$

(📱 03-379 4560; www.thegeorge.com; 50 Park
Tce; r $356-379, ste $574-761; P@🛜) 🏴 The
George has 53 handsomely decorated rooms
within a defiantly 1970s-looking building
on the fringe of Hagley Park. Discreet staff
attend to every whim, and ritzy features
include huge TVs, luxury toiletries, glossy
magazines and two highly rated in-house
restaurants – Pescatore and 50 Bistro.

Heritage Christchurch
HOTEL $$$

(📱 03-983 4800; www.heritagehotels.co.nz; 28-30
Cathedral Sq; ste $235-440; 🛜) 🏴 Standing
grandly on Cathedral Sq while all around it is
in ruins, the 1909 Old Government Building
owes its survival to a thorough strengthening

Central Christchurch

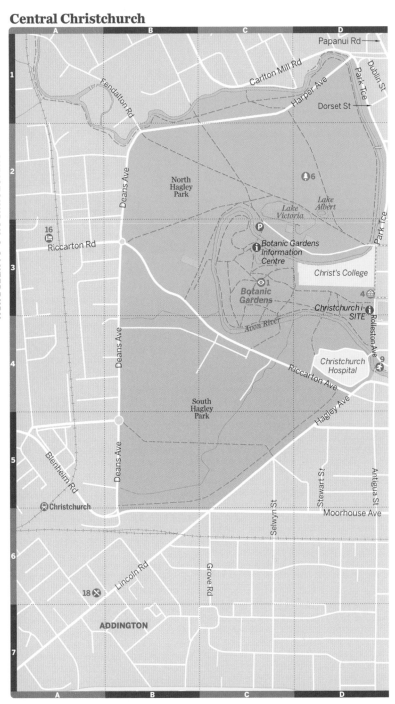

Papanui Rd

Carlton Mill Rd

Fendalton Rd

Harper Ave

Dublin St

Park Tce

Dorset St

North Hagley Park

Lake Albert

Lake Victoria

16

Riccarton Rd

Deans Ave

Botanic Gardens Information Centre

Christ's College

Botanic Gardens

1

4

Christchurch i-SITE

Rolleston Ave

Avon River

Christchurch Hospital

9

Riccarton Ave

South Hagley Park

Hagley Ave

Deans Ave

Stewart St

Antigua St

Blenheim Rd

Christchurch

Selwyn St

Moorhouse Ave

Deans Ave

Lincoln Rd

Grove Rd

18

ADDINGTON

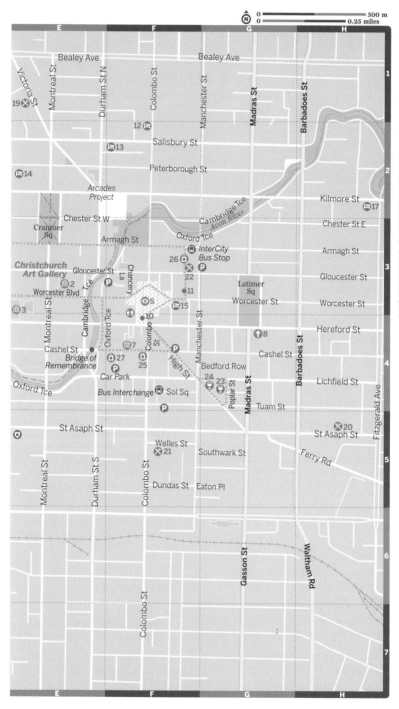

Central Christchurch

⊙ Top Sights
1 Botanic Gardens C3
2 Christchurch Art Gallery E3

⊙ Sights
3 Arts Centre E3
4 Canterbury Museum D3
5 Cathedral Square F3
6 Hagley Park D2
7 Quake City F4
8 Transitional Cathedral G4

⊕ Activities, Courses & Tours
9 Antigua Boat Sheds D4
   Christchurch Bike &
      Walking Tours .... (see 9)
10 Christchurch Free Tours F4
11 Tram F3

⊜ Sleeping
12 CentrePoint on Colombo F2
13 Focus Motel F2
14 George E2
15 Heritage Christchurch F3

16 Lorenzo Motor Inn A3
17 Pomeroy's on Kilmore H2

⊗ Eating
18 Addington Coffee Co-op A6
19 King of Snake E1
20 Lotus Heart H5
21 Supreme Supreme F5
22 Twenty Seven Steps F3

⊙ Drinking & Nightlife
23 Dux Central G4
   Pomeroy's Old Brewery Inn .... (see 17)
24 Smash Palace G4

⊙ Shopping
25 Ballantynes F4
26 New Regent St F3
27 Re:START Mall F4

⊙ Information
   Christchurch DOC Visitor
      Centre .... (see 27)
   Visitor Kiosk .... (see 27)

when it was converted to a hotel in the 1990s. After a three-year postearthquake restoration its spacious suites are more elegant than ever. All have full kitchens.

✕ Eating

★ Supreme Supreme   CAFE $
(☏03-365 0445; www.supremesupreme.co.nz; 10 Welles St; breakfast $7-18, lunch $10-20; ⊙7am-4pm Mon-Fri, 8am-4pm Sat & Sun; ✐) With so much to love, where to start? Perhaps with a kimchi Bloody Mary, a chocolate-fish milkshake, or maybe just an exceptional espresso alongside ancient-grain muesli or pulled corn-beef hash. One of NZ's original and best coffee roasters comes to the party with a right-now cafe of splendid style, form and function.

Addington Coffee Co-op   CAFE $
(☏03-943 1662; www.addingtoncoffee.org.nz; 297 Lincoln Rd; meals $8-21; ⊙7.30am-4pm Mon-Fri, 9am-4pm Sat & Sun; 🥄✐) You will find one of Christchurch's biggest and best cafes packed to the rafters most days. A compact shop selling fair-trade gifts jostles for attention with delicious cakes, gourmet pies and the legendary house breakfasts (until 2pm). An on-site launderette completes the deal for busy travellers.

★ Bodhi Tree   BURMESE $$
(☏03-377 6808; www.bodhitree.co.nz; 399 Ilam Rd, Bryndwr; dishes $13-21; ⊙6-10pm Tue-Sat; ✐) Bodhi Tree has been wowing locals with the nuanced flavours of Burmese cuisine for more than a decade. Its feel-good food comes in sharing-sized dishes and sings with zing. Standouts include *le pet thoke* (pickled tea-leaf salad) and *ameyda nut* (slow-cooked beef curry).

Lotus Heart   VEGETARIAN $$
(☏03-377 2727; www.thelotusheart.co.nz; 363 St Asaph St; mains $13-25; ⊙7.30am-3pm Tue-Sun & 5-9pm Fri & Sat; ✐) 🌱 Run by students of Sri Chinmoy, this vegetarian eatery serves curry, pizza, wraps, burgers and freshly squeezed organic juices. Organic, vegan and gluten-free options abound, and there's an interesting gift and music shop on-site.

★ Twenty Seven Steps   MODERN NZ $$$
(☏03-366 2727; www.twentysevensteps.co.nz; 16 New Regent St; mains $30-40; ⊙5pm-late Tue-Sat) Upstairs on the Edwardian New Regent St strip, the pared-back interior of this elegant restaurant puts the focus firmly on a menu showcasing local produce. Mainstays include modern renditions of lamb, beef, venison and seafood, but there's also outstanding risotto and desserts such as caramelised lemon tart.

King of Snake

ASIAN $$$

(☑ 03-365 7363; www.kingofsnake.co.nz; 145 Victoria St; mains $27-43; ☺ 11am-late Mon-Fri, 4pm-late Sat & Sun) Dark wood, gold tiles and purple skull-patterned wallpaper fill this hip restaurant and cocktail bar with just the right amount of sinister opulence. The exciting menu gainfully plunders the cuisines of Asia to delicious, if pricey, effect.

Drinking & Nightlife

★ Smash Palace

BAR

(☑ 03-366 5369; www.thesmashpalace.co.nz; 172 High St; ☺ 4pm-late Mon-Fri, noon-late Sat & Sun) Epitomising the spirit of transience, tenacity and number-eight wire that Christchurch is now known for, this deliberately downcycled and ramshackle beer garden is an intoxicating mix of grease-monkey garage, trailer-park trash, and proto-hipster hang-out complete with a psychedelic school bus, edible garden and blooming roses. There's craft beer, chips and cereal, and burgers made from scratch ($11 to $15).

★ Pomeroy's Old Brewery Inn

PUB

(☑ 03-365 1523; www.pomspub.co.nz; 292 Kilmore St; ☺ 3-11pm Tue-Thu, noon-11pm Fri-Sun) For fans of great beer, there's no better place than Pomeroy's for supping a drop or two alongside a plate of proper pork crackling. Among this British-style pub's many other endearing features are regular live music, a snug, sunny courtyard and Victoria's Kitchen, serving comforting pub food (mains $24 to $30). The newest addition, pretty **Little Pom's** cafe, serves super-fine fare (meals $14 to $22) until mid-afternoon.

Dux Central

BAR

(☑ 03-943 7830; www.duxcentral.co.nz; 6 Poplar St; ☺ 11am-late) Pumping a whole lot of heart back into the flattened High St precinct, the epic new Dux comprises a brew bar serving its own and other crafty drops, the Emerald Room wine bar, Upper Dux restaurant and the Poplar Social Club cocktail bar, all within the confines of a lovingly restored old building.

Revival

BAR

(☑ 03-379 9559; www.revivalbar.co.nz; 92-96 Victoria St; ☺ 3pm-late Mon-Thu, noon-late Fri-Sun) Revival is the hippest of Christchurch's shipping container bars. Expect regular DJs and a funky lounge area dotted with a quirky collection of automotive rear ends and vintage steamer trunks.

Shopping

★ Tannery

SHOPPING CENTRE

(www.thetannery.co.nz; 3 Garlands Rd, Woolston; ☺ 10am-5pm Mon-Wed, Fri & Sat, to 8pm Thu) In a city mourning the loss of its heritage, this postearthquake conversion of a 19th-century tannery couldn't be more welcome. The Victorian buildings have been jooshed up in period style, and filled with boutique shops selling everything from books to fashion to surfboards. Don't miss the woolly hats. Nonshoppers can slink off to the Brewery or catch a movie in the brand-new cinemas.

Re:START Mall

MALL

(www.restart.org.nz; Cashel St; ☺ 10am-5pm; 🛜) This labyrinth of shipping containers was the first retail 'mall' to reopen in the CBD postquakes. With cafes, food trucks, shops and people-watching opportunities, it remains a pleasant place to hang out, particularly on a sunny day. At the time of writing, there were no plans for the Re:START to disappear any time soon.

New Regent St

MALL

(www.newregentstreet.co.nz) A forerunner to the modern mall, this pretty little stretch of pastel Spanish Mission–style shops was described as NZ's most beautiful street when it was completed in 1932. Fully restored postearthquake, it's once again a delightful place to stroll and peruse the tiny galleries, gift shops and cafes.

Ballantynes

DEPARTMENT STORE

(www.ballantynes.com; cnr Colombo & Cashel Sts; ☺ 9am-5pm) A venerable Christchurch department store selling men's and women's fashions, cosmetics, travel goods and speciality NZ gifts. Fashionistas should check out the Contemporary Lounge upstairs.

ℹ Information

EMERGENCY

Ambulance, Fire & Police (☑ 111)

USEFUL WEBSITES

CERA (www.cera.govt.nz) The Canterbury Earthquake Recovery Authority has the lowdown on rebuild plans and status updates.

Christchurch City Council (www.ccc.govt.nz) The city council's official website.

MEDICAL SERVICES

Christchurch Hospital (☑ 03-364 0640, emergency dept 03-364 0270; www.cdhb.

Waipara Valley
CLAVER CARROLL/GETTY IMAGES ©

govt.nz; 2 Riccarton Ave) Has a 24-hour emergency department.

Urgent Pharmacy (☑ 03-366 4439; cnr Bealey Ave & Colombo St; ⊙ 6-11pm Mon-Fri, 9am-11pm Sat & Sun) Located beside the 24 Hour Surgery.

TOURIST INFORMATION

Christchurch DOC Visitor Centre (☑ 03-379 4082; www.doc.govt.nz; Cashel St, Re:START Mall; ⊙ 10am-5pm) Offers countrywide information and Great Walk bookings. A change in premises was on the cards at the time of writing; ring or check the website for updates.

Christchurch i-SITE (☑ 03-379 9629; www.christchurchnz.com; Botanic Gardens, Rolleston Ave; ⊙ 8.30am-5pm, extended hours in summer) This ever-helpful and eternally busy i-SITE also now has an outpost in the Re:START Mall, open daily from November to March.

Visitor Kiosk (☑ 03-379 9629; www.christchurchnz.com; Cashel Mall, Re:START Mall; ⊙ 8.30am-5pm Nov-Apr) Outpost of the ever-helpful and eternally busy i-SITE.

❶ Getting There & Away

AIR

Christchurch Airport (CHC; ☑ 03-358 5029; www.christchurchairport.co.nz; 30 Durey Rd) is the South Island's main international gateway, with excellent facilities including baggage storage, hire-car counters, ATMs, foreign-exchange offices and an i-SITE visitor information centre.

❶ Getting Around

CAR & MOTORCYCLE

Most major car- and campervan-rental companies have offices in Christchurch, as do numerous smaller local companies. Operators with national networks often want cars from Christchurch to be returned to Auckland because most renters travel in the opposite direction, so you may find a cheaper price on a northbound route.

Local options include the following:

Ace Rental Cars (☑ 03-360 3270; www.acerentalcars.co.nz; 20 Abros Pl, Burnside)

First Choice (www.firstchoice.co.nz)

New Zealand Motorcycle Rentals & Tours (☑ 09-486 2472; www.nzbike.com)

Omega Rental Cars (☑ 03-377 4558; www.omegarentalcars.com; 252 Lichfield St)

Pegasus Rental Cars (☑ 03-358 5890; www.rentalcars.co.nz; 34b Sheffield Cres, Burnside)

Waipara Valley

◉ Sights

★ **Pegasus Bay** WINERY
(☑ 03-314 6869; www.pegasusbay.com; Stockgrove Rd; ⊙ tastings 10am-5pm) It's fitting that Waipara Valley's premier winery should have the loveliest setting and one of Canterbury's best restaurants (mains $36 to $44, serving noon to 4pm Thursday to Monday). Beautiful gardens set the scene but it's the contemporary NZ menu and luscious wines that steal the show. Pétanque available upon request.

Black Estate WINERY
(☑ 03-314 6085; www.blackestate.co.nz; 614 Omihi Rd/SH1; ⊙ 10am-5pm Wed-Sun, daily Dec-Jan) The sharpest of Waipara's wineries architecturally, this striking black barn overlooking the valley is home to some excellent wine, and food that champions local producers (mains $25 to $40). As well as the region's common cool-climate wines, look out for its interesting pinot/chardonnay rosé and seductive chenin blanc.

Brew Moon BREWERY
(☑ 03-314 8036; www.brewmoon.co.nz; 12 Markham St, Amberley; ⊙ 3pm-late Wed-Fri, noon-late Sat & Sun) The variety of craft beers available to taste at this wee brewery never wanes. Stop in to fill a rigger (flagon) to take away, or sup an ale with a platter or a pizza (food from 3pm).

Sleeping & Eating

Old Glenmark Vicarage B&B $$$
(☑03-314 6775; www.glenmarkvicarage.co.nz; 161 Church Rd, Waipara; d $230, barn d $210; 🛜🐾) There are two divine options in this beautifully restored century-old vicarage: cosy up with bed and breakfast in the main house, or lounge around in the character-filled, converted barn that sleeps up to five. The beautiful gardens and swimming pool are a blessed bonus.

★Little Vintage Espresso CAFE $
(20 Markham St, Amberley; brunch $8-18; ⊙7.30am-4.30pm Mon-Sat) This little cracker of a cafe just off SH1 serves up the best coffee in town with food to match. High-quality, contemporary sandwiches, slices and cakes are gobbled up by locals and tourists alike.

Pukeko Junction CAFE, DELI $$
(☑03-314 8834; www.pukekojunction.co.nz; 458 Ashworths Rd/SH1, Leithfield; mains $15-21; ⊙9am-4.30pm; 🐾) A deservedly popular roadside pit stop, this cafe in Leithfield (south of Amberley) serves delicious baked goods including gourmet sausage rolls and lamb shank pies. As well as arts and crafts, the shop next door stocks an excellent selection of local wine.

Arthur's Pass

◉ Sights

★Castle Hill/Kura Tawhiti LANDMARK
Scattered across lush paddocks around 33km from Springfield, these limestone formations are so odd they were named 'treasure from a distant land' by early Māori. A car park (with toilets) provides easy access on foot into the strange rock garden, favoured by rock climbers and photographers.

Arthur's Pass National Park NATIONAL PARK
(www.doc.govt.nz) Pick up a copy of DOC's *Discover Arthur's Pass* booklet to read about popular walks through this national park, including: **Arthur's Pass Walkway**, a reasonably easy track from the village to the Dobson Memorial at the summit of the pass (2½ hours return); the one-hour return walk to **Devils Punchbowl** falls; and the steep walk to beautiful views at **Temple Basin** (three hours return). More challenging, full-day options include **Bealey Spur** track and the classic summit hike to **Avalanche Peak** (p39).

The park's many multiday trails are mostly valley routes with saddle climbs in between, such as **Goat Pass** and **Cass-Lagoon Saddles Tracks**, both two-day options. These and the park's longer tracks require previous tramping experience as flooding can make the rivers dangerous and the weather is extremely changeable. Always seek advice from DOC before setting out.

Sleeping

Camping is possible near the basic **Avalanche Creek Shelter** (adult/child $6/3) opposite the DOC centre, where there's running water, a sink, tables and a toilet. You can also camp for free at **Klondyke Corner** or **Hawdon Shelter**, 8km and 24km south of Arthur's Pass respectively, where facilities are limited to toilets and stream water for boiling.

Mountain House YHA HOSTEL $
(☑03-318 9258; www.trampers.co.nz; 83 Main Rd; dm $31-34, s/d/unit $74/86/155; 🛜) Spread around the village, this excellent suite of accommodation includes a well-kept hostel, two upmarket motel units and two three-bedroom cottages with log fires ($340, for up to eight people). The enthusiastic manager runs a tight ship and can provide extensive local tramping information.

Arthur's Pass Village B&B B&B $$
(☑021 394 776; www.arthurspass.org.nz; 72 School Tce; d $140-160; 🛜) This lovingly restored former railway cottage is now a cosy B&B, complete with two guest bedrooms (share bathroom), free-range bacon and eggs, and freshly baked bread for breakfast, and the company of interesting owners. Home-cooked dinners are also available ($35). Ask about the scorched floorboard.

Arthur's Pass Alpine Motel MOTEL $$
(☑03-318 9233; www.apam.co.nz; 52 Main Rd; d $125-150; 🛜) On the southern approach to the village, this cabin-style motel complex combines the homely charms of yesteryear with the beauty of double-glazing and the advice of active, enthusiastic hosts.

Wilderness Lodge LODGE $$$
(☑03-318 9246; www.wildernesslodge.co.nz; Cora Lynn Rd, Bealey; s $499-749, d $778-1178; 🛜) 🌿 For tranquillity and natural grandeur, this mid-size alpine lodge tucked into beech forest just off the highway takes some beating. It's a class act with a focus on immersive, nature-based experiences. Two daily guided activities (such as tramping and kayaking) are included in the tariff along with dinner and breakfast.

Eating

Arthur's Pass Store & Cafe
CAFE $

(85 Main Rd; breakfast & lunch $7-24; ⊘ 8am-5pm; ☎) You want it, this is your best chance, with odds-on for egg sandwiches, hot chips, good coffee, petrol and basic groceries.

ⓘ Information

DOC Arthur's Pass Visitor Centre (☎ 03-318 9211; www.doc.govt.nz; 80 Main Rd; ⊘ 8.30pm-4.30pm) Displays include ecological information and the history of Arthur's Pass. Helpful staff provide advice on suitable tramps and the all-important weather forecast. Detailed route guides and topographical maps will further aid your safety, as will hire of a locator beacon and logging your trip details on AdventureSmart (www.adventuresmart.org.nz) via the on-site computer.

Methven

🏃 Activities

Methven Heliski
SKIING

(☎ 03-302 8108; www.methvenheli.co.nz; Main St; 5-run day trips $1045) Epic guided, all-inclusive backcountry ski trips, featuring five runs averaging drops of 750 to 1000 vertical metres.

Aoraki Balloon Safaris
BALLOONING

(☎ 03-302 8172; www.nzballooning.com; flights $385) Early-morning combo of snowcapped peaks and a breakfast with bubbly.

Skydiving Kiwis
SKYDIVING

(☎ 0800 359 549; www.skydivingkiwis.com; Ashburton Airport, Seafield Rd) Offers tandem jumps from 6,000ft ($235), 9,000ft ($285) and 12,000ft ($335).

🛏 Sleeping

Alpenhorn Chalet
HOSTEL $

(☎ 03-302 8779; www.alpenhorn.co.nz; 44 Allen St; dm $30, d $65-85; @ ☎) This small, inviting home has a leafy conservatory housing an indoor spa pool, a log fire, and complimentary espresso coffee. Bedrooms are spacious and brightly coloured, with lots of warm, natural wood; one double room has an en suite bathroom.

Rakaia Gorge
Camping Ground
CAMPGROUND $

(☎ 03-302 9353; 6686 Arundel-Rakaia Gorge Rd; sites per adult/child under 12yr $8.50/free) There are no powered sites and only toilets, showers and a small kitchen shelter, but don't let that put you off. This is the best camp-ing ground for miles, perched handsomely above the ultrablue Rakaia River, and a good base for exploring the area. Amenities closed May to October.

Redwood Lodge
HOSTEL, LODGE $$

(☎ 03-302 8964; www.redwoodlodge.co.nz; 3 Wayne Pl; s $55-65, d $104-149; @ ☎) Expect a warm, woolly welcome and no dorms at this charming and peaceful family-friendly lodge. Most rooms are en suite, and bigger rooms can be reconfigured to accommodate families. The large shared lounge is ideal for resting ski-weary limbs.

Whitestone Cottages
RENTAL HOUSE $$$

(☎ 03-928 8050; www.whitestonecottages.co.nz; 3016 Methven Hwy; cottages $175-255) When you just want to spread out, cook a meal, do your laundry and have your own space, these four large free-standing houses in leafy grounds are just the ticket. Each sleeps six in two en suite bedrooms. Base rates are for two; each extra person is $35.

✕ Eating

Cafe 131
CAFE $

(131 Main St; meals $10-20; ⊘ 7.30am-5pm; ☎) Polished timber and lead-light windows lend atmosphere to this conservative but reliable local favourite. Highlights include good coffee, tasty all-day breakfasts and admirable home-baking, with a tipple on offer should you fancy it. Free wi-fi makes this the town's de facto internet cafe.

★ Dubliner
RESTAURANT $$

(www.dubliner.co.nz; 116 Main St; meals $26-34; ⊘ 4pm-late) This authentically Irish bar and restaurant is housed in Methven's lovingly restored old post office. Great food includes pizza, Irish stew and other hearty fare suitable for washing down with a pint of craft beer.

Aqua
JAPANESE $$

(☎ 03-302 8335; 112 Main St; mains $13-21; ⊘ 5-9pm, closed Nov) A ski-season stalwart with unpredictable summer hours (so ring ahead), this tiny restaurant sports kimono-clad waitresses and traditional Japanese cuisine including yakisoba (fried noodles), ramen (noodle soup) and *izakaya*-style small plates to share with ice-cold beer or warming sake.

ⓘ Information

Methven i-SITE (☎ 03-302 8955; www.methvenmthutt.co.nz; 160 Main St; ⊘ 9.30am-5pm daily Jul-Sep, 9am-5pm Mon-Fri, 10am-3pm

Sat & Sun Oct-Jun; ☎) Ask staff here about local walks and other activities, then enjoy the free art gallery and the hands-on NZ Alpine & Agriculture Encounter (adult/child $12.70/7.50).

Medical Centre (☑ 03-302 8105; The Square, Main St; ☺ 8.30am-5.30pm)

Geraldine

◉ Sights & Activities

Geraldine Museum MUSEUM
(5 Cox St; ☺ 10am-3pm Mon-Sat, 12.30-3pm Sun) FREE Occupying the photogenic Town Board Office building (1885), and sporting a new side wing, this cute little museum tells the town's story with an eclectic mix of exhibits, including an extensive collection of photographs.

Vintage Car & Machinery Museum MUSEUM
(☑ 03-693 8756; 178 Talbot St; adult/child $10/free; ☺ 9.30am-4pm Oct-May, 10am-4pm Sat & Sun Jun-Sep) You don't have to be a rev-head to enjoy this vintage car collection featuring a 1907 De Dion-Bouton and a gleaming 1926 Bentley. There's also a purpose-built Daimler used for the 1954 royal tour, plus some very nice Jags, 1970s muscle cars and all sorts of farm machinery.

Big Rock Canyons ADVENTURE SPORTS
(☑ 0800 244 762; www.bigrockcanyons.co.nz; ☺ Oct-Apr) Offers slippy, slidey day-long adventures in the Kaumira Canyon ($360) near Geraldine, as well as in five other canyons with varying degrees of difficulty.

⎸⎺⎸ Sleeping

Rawhiti Backpackers HOSTEL $
(☑ 03-693 8252; www.rawhitibackpackers.co.nz; 27 Hewlings St; dm/s/d $34/50/78; ☎) On a hillside on the edge of town, this former maternity hospital is now a sunny and spacious hostel with good communal areas, comfortable rooms, a lemon tree and two cute cats. Bikes are available to borrow.

Geraldine Kiwi Holiday Park HOLIDAY PARK, MOTEL $
(☑ 03-693 8147; www.geraldineholidaypark.co.nz; 39 Hislop St; sites $34-39, d $52-135; @ ☎) 🐾 This top-notch holiday park is set amid well-established parkland, two minutes' walk from the high street. Tidy accommodation ranges from budget cabins to plusher motel units, plus there's a TV room and playground.

Scenic Route Motor Lodge MOTEL $$
(☑ 03-693 9700; www.motelscenicroute.co.nz; 28 Waihi Tce; d $135-155; ☎) There's a vaguely heritage feel to this stone and timber motel, but the modern units have double-glazing, flat-screen TVs and even stylish wallpaper. Larger studios have spa baths.

✕ Eating

★ **Talbot Forest Cheese** DELI $
(www.talbotforestcheese.co.nz; Four Peaks Plaza, Talbot Rd; cheeses $5-10; ☺ 9am-5pm; ⎘) This little shop not only showcases the cheeses made on-site (including fine Parmesan and Gruyère), it doubles as a deli with all you need for a tasty picnic.

Verde CAFE $
(☑ 03-693 9616; 45 Talbot St; mains $11-18; ☺ 9am-4pm; ⎘) Down the lane beside the old post office and set in beautiful gardens, this excellent cafe is easily the best of Geraldine's eateries. It's just a shame that it's not open for dinner.

❶ Information

Geraldine Visitor Information Centre (☑ 03-693 1101; www.southcanterbury.org.nz; 38 Waihi Tce; ☺ 8am-5.30pm) The information centre is located inside the Kiwi Country visitor complex. See also www.gogeraldine.co.nz.

Lake Tekapo

◉ Sights

Church of the Good Shepherd CHURCH
(Pioneer Dr; ☺ 9am-5pm) The prime disgorging point for tour buses, this interdenominational lakeside church was built of stone and oak in 1935. A picture window behind the altar gives churchgoers a distractingly divine view of lake and mountain majesty; needless to say, it's a firm favourite for weddings.

🏃 Activities

Mackenzie Alpine Horse Trekking HORSE RIDING
(☑ 0800 628 269; www.maht.co.nz; Godley Peaks Rd; 1hr/2hr/day $70/110/310) Located on the road to Mt John, these folks run various treks taking in the area's amazing scenery.

Tekapo Springs SPA
(☑ 03-680 6550; www.tekaposprings.co.nz; 6 Lakeside Dr; adult/child pools $22/13, ice-skating $16/12; ☺ 10am-9pm) Turn up the heat from the 36°C pool, to the 38°C and 40°C

pools, soaking in the thermal goodness in landscaped surrounds overlooking the lake. There's a steam room and sauna, along with a day spa offering various indulgences including massage.

👉 Tours

Earth & Sky
TOUR

(📞03-680 6960; www.earthandsky.co.nz; SH8) 🏄
If you've ever wanted to tour an observatory and survey the night sky, this is the place to do it. Nightly tours head up to the University of Canterbury's observatory on Mt John. Day tours are given on demand in winter, while in summer there's usually a guide at the observatory from midday to 3pm.

Air Safaris
SCENIC FLIGHTS

(📞03-680 6880; www.airsafaris.co.nz; SH8)
Awe-inspiring views of Aoraki/Mt Cook National Park's peaks and glaciers are offered on the 'Grand Traverse' fixed-wing flight (adult/child $360/230), and there are other options including similar trips in a helicopter.

🛏 Sleeping

Tekapo Motels & Holiday Park
HOLIDAY PARK, MOTEL $

(📞03-680 6825; www.laketekapo-accommodation.co.nz; 2 Lakeside Dr; sites $34-44, dm $30-32, d $90-110; 🖥) Supremely situated on terraced, lakefront grounds, this place has something for everyone. Backpackers get the cosy, log-cabin-style lodge, while others can enjoy cute

Kiwi bachs, basic cabins, and smart en suite units with particularly good views.

YHA Lake Tekapo
HOSTEL $

(📞03-680 6857; www.yha.co.nz; 3 Simpson Lane; sites per person $20, dm $33-38, d $99-104; @ 🖥)
🏄 Older-style, tidy and well-maintained hostel with million-dollar views of Lake Tekapo. Snuggle around the fire in winter, or chill out by the lake in summer.

★ Lake Tekapo Lodge
B&B $$$

(📞03-680 6566; www.laketekapolodge.co.nz; 24 Aorangi Cres; r $300-450; 🖥) This fabulously designed, luxurious B&B is filled to the brim with covetable contemporary Kiwi art, and boasts painterly views of the lake and mountains from the sumptuous rooms and lounge.

🍴 Eating & Drinking

★ Astro Café
CAFE $

(Mt John University Observatory; mains $7-12; ⏰9am-5pm) This glass-walled pavilion atop Mt John has spectacular 360-degree views across the entire Mackenzie Basin – quite possibly one of the planet's best locations for a cafe. Tuck into bagels with local salmon, or fresh ham-off-the-bone sandwiches; the coffee and cake are good, too.

Kohan
JAPANESE $$

(📞03-680 6688; www.kohannz.com; SH8; dishes $8-20, mains $19-30; ⏰11am-2pm daily, 6-9pm Mon-Sat) With all the aesthetic charm of an office cafeteria, this is still one of Tekapo's best dining options, both for its distracting lake views, and its authentic Japanese food including fresh-as-a-daisy salmon sashimi.

Mackenzie's Bar & Grill
BAR

(SH8; ⏰11.30am-late Mon-Fri, 10am-late Sat & Sun) While full immersion on the menu front is not necessarily advisable, this tidy gastro-pub-style establishment is a safe bet for a few cold ones and some bar snacks. The views are grand, particularly outside from the patio and garden in front.

ℹ Information

Kiwi Treasures & Information Centre (📞03-680 6686; SH8; ⏰8am-5.30pm Mon-Fri, to 6pm Sat & Sun) This little gift shop doubles as the post office and info centre with local maps and advice, plus bookings for local activities and national bus services. See also www.tekapotourism.co.nz.

Church of the Good Shephard (p91), Lake Tekapo

Aoraki/Mt Cook National Park

◉ Sights

★ Aoraki/Mt Cook National Park Visitor Centre MUSEUM

(☑ 03-435 1186; www.doc.govt.nz; 1 Larch Grove; ☉ 8.30am-4.30pm, to 5pm Oct-Apr) **FREE** Arguably the best DOC visitor centre in NZ. It not only dispatches all necessary information and advice on tramping routes and weather conditions, it also houses excellent displays on the park's natural and human history. It's a fabulous place to commune with the wilderness, even on a rainy day.

Sir Edmund Hillary Alpine Centre MUSEUM

(www.hermitage.co.nz; The Hermitage, Terrace Rd; adult/child $20/10; ☉ 7am-8.30pm Oct-Mar, 8am-7pm Apr-Sep) This multimedia museum opened just three weeks before the January 2008 death of the man widely regarded as the greatest New Zealander of all time. Sir Ed's commentary tracks were recorded only a few months before he died.

🏃 Activities

★ Sealy Tarns Track TRAMPING

The walk to Sealy Tarns (three to four hours return) branches off the Kea Point Track

and continues up the ridge to Mueller Hut (dorm $36), a comfortable 28-bunk hut with gas, cooking facilities and long-drop toilets.

Hooker Valley Track TRAMPING

Perhaps the best of the area's day walks, this track (three hours return from Mt Cook Village) heads up the Hooker Valley and crosses three swing bridges to the Stocking Stream and the terminus of the Hooker Glacier. After the second swing bridge, Aoraki/Mt Cook totally dominates the valley, and you may see icebergs floating in Hooker Lake.

Southern Alps Guiding OUTDOOR ADVENTURE

(☑ 03-435 1890; www.mtcook.com; Old Mountaineers' Cafe, 3 Larch Grove Rd) Offers mountaineering instruction and guiding, plus three- to four-hour helihiking trips on Tasman Glacier year-round ($495). From June to October heliskiers can head up Tasman Glacier for a 10km to 12km downhill run (three runs, from $895). There's also a ski-plane option (two runs, from $895).

👉 Tours

Mount Cook Ski Planes SCENIC FLIGHTS

(☑ 03-430 8026; www.mtcookskiplanes.com) Based at Mt Cook Airport, this outfit offers 45-minute (adult/child $425/310) and 55-minute (adult/child $560/425) flights, both with snow landings. Flight-seeing

DON'T MISS

TASMAN GLACIER

At 29km long and up to 4km wide, the Tasman Glacier (www.doc.govt.nz) is the largest of NZ's glaciers, but it's melting fast, losing hundreds of metres from its length each year. It is also melting from the surface down, shrinking around 150m in depth since it was first surveyed in 1891. In its lower section the melts have exposed rocks, stones and boulders, which form a solid unsightly mass on top of the ice. Despite this considerable shrinkage, at its thickest point the ice is still estimated to be over 600m deep.

Tasman Lake, at the foot of the glacier, started to form only in the early 1970s and now stretches to 4km. The ongoing effects of climate change are expected to extend it to 8km within the next 20 years. The lake is covered by a maze of huge icebergs which are continuously being sheared off the glacier's terminal face. On 22 February 2011 the Christchurch earthquake caused a 1.3km long, 300m high, 30-million-ton chunk of ice to break off, causing 3.5m waves to roll into the tourist boats on the lake at the time (no one was injured). You can kayak on Tasman Lake with **Glacier Kayaking** (☑ 03-435 1890; www.mtcook.com; Old Mountaineers' Cafe, Bowen Dr; per person $155; ☉ Oct-Apr).

In the glacier's last major advance (17,000 years ago), the glacier crept south far enough to carve out Lake Pukaki. A later advance did not reach out to the valley sides, so there's a gap between the outer valley walls and the lateral moraines of this later advance. The unsealed Tasman Valley Rd, which branches off Mt Cook Rd 800m south of Mt Cook Village, travels through this gap. From the Blue Lakes shelter, 8km along the road, the **Tasman Glacier View Track** (30 minutes return) climbs interminable steps to an aptly rewarding viewpoint on the moraine wall, with a side trip to Blue Lakes on the way.

Aoraki/Mt Cook National Park

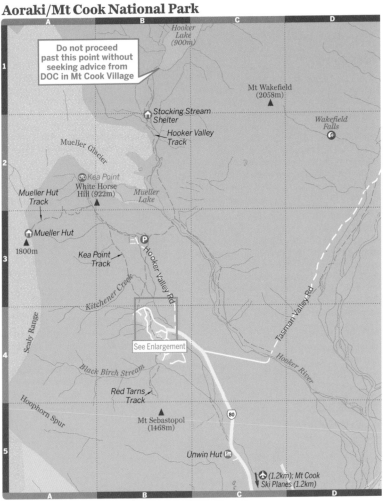

Aoraki/Mt Cook National Park

◉ Sights
1 Aoraki/Mt Cook National
 Park Visitor Centre E4
2 Sir Edmund Hillary Alpine
 Centre E4

✦ Activities, Courses & Tours
 Glacier Explorers .... (see 5)
 Southern Alps
 Guiding .... (see 6)

⌷ Sleeping
3 Aoraki Court Motel F5
4 Aoraki/Mt Cook Alpine Lodge E5
5 Hermitage E4

✖ Eating
6 Old Mountaineers' Cafe E4

◗ Drinking & Nightlife
7 Chamois Bar & Grill F5

without a landing is a cheaper option; try the 25-minute Mini Tasman trip (adult/ child $245/200) or 45-minute Alpine Wonderland (adult/child $310/250).

room $180/100; @ 🛜) 🚩 On Lake Pukaki's northern shore, 22km south of the Mt Cook Village, this is the nearest fully equipped campground to the national park. Features include cabins and motel units, a bunk room and a cafe.

★ Aoraki/Mt Cook Alpine Lodge LODGE $$

(🖉 03-435 1860; www.aorakialpinelodge.co.nz; Bowen Dr; d $169-240; 🛜) This lovely modern lodge has en suite rooms, including some suitable for families and two with kitchenettes; most have views. The huge lounge and kitchen area also has a superb mountain outlook, as does the barbecue area – a rather inspiring spot to sizzle your dinner.

Hermitage HOTEL $$$

(🖉 03-435 1809; www.hermitage.co.nz; Terrace Rd; r $215-510; @ 🛜) Completely dominating Mt Cook Village, this famous hotel offers awesome mountain views. While the corridors in some of the older wings can seem a little hospital-like, all of the rooms have been renovated to a reasonable standard.

Aoraki Court Motel MOTEL $$$

(🖉 03-435 1111; www.aorakicourt.co.nz; 26 Bowen Dr; d $185-265) While it wouldn't command these prices elsewhere, this clump of modern motel units is sharp, with good views. Feature wallpaper sharpens up the decor, and the tiled bathrooms have designery touches.

🍴 Eating & Drinking

Old Mountaineers' Cafe CAFE $$

(www.mtcook.com; Bowen Dr; breakfast $10-15, lunch $14-26, dinner $18-35; ⊙10am-9pm daily Nov-Apr, Tue-Sun May & Jul-Oct; 🛜) 🚩 Encouraging lingering with books, memorabilia and mountain views through picture windows, the village's best eatery also supports local and organic suppliers through a menu sporting salmon and bacon pies, cooked breakfasts, burgers and pizza.

Chamois Bar & Grill PUB

(www.mountcookbackpackers.co.nz; Bowen Dr; ⊙4pm-late) Upstairs in Mt Cook Backpacker Lodge, this large bar offers pub grub (meals $15 to $30), a pool table, a big-screen TV and the occasional live gig, but the views are its best feature.

❶ Information

The DOC Visitor Centre (p93) is the best source of local information. The nearest ATM and supermarket are in Twizel.

Glacier Explorers BOAT TOUR

(🖉 03-435 1641; www.glacierexplorers.com; The Hermitage, Terrace Rd; adult/child $155/77.50; ⊙Sep-May) Head out on the terminal lake of the Tasman Glacier for this small-boat tour, which gets up close and personal with old icebergs and crazy moraines. Includes a short walk. Book at the activities desk at the Hermitage hotel.

🛏 Sleeping

Glentanner Park Centre HOLIDAY PARK $

(🖉 03-435 1855; www.glentanner.co.nz; Mt Cook Rd; sites $22-25, dm $32, units with/without bath-

Queenstown & Wanaka

With a cinematic background of mountains and lakes, and a 'what can we think of next?' array of adventure activities, it's little wonder Queenstown tops the itineraries of many travellers. Wanaka – Queenstown's less flashy cousin – has great restaurants, bars and outdoor adventures on tap.

Queenstown

Surrounded by the soaring indigo heights of the Remarkables and framed by the meandering coves of Lake Wakatipu, Queenstown is a right show-off. Looking like a small town, but displaying the energy of a small city, it wears its 'Global Adventure Capital' badge proudly, and most visitors take the time to do crazy things that they've never done before. No one's ever visited and said, 'I'm bored'.

◉ Sights

Lake Wakatipu LAKE

Shaped like a perfect cartoon thunderbolt, this gorgeous lake has a 212km shoreline and reaches a depth of 379m (the average depth is over 320m). Five rivers flow into it but only one (the Kawarau) flows out, making it prone to sometimes quite dramatic floods.

Queenstown Gardens PARK

(Park St) Set on its own little tongue of land framing Queenstown Bay, this pretty park was laid out in 1876 by those garden-loving Victorians as a place to promenade. The clothes may have changed (they've certainly shrunk), but people still flock to this leafy peninsula to stroll, picnic and laze about. Less genteel types head straight for the frisbee golf course.

Kiwi Birdlife Park ZOO

(☑03-442 8059; www.kiwibird.co.nz; Brecon St; adult/child $45/23; ◷9am-5pm, shows 11am & 3pm) These five acres are home to 10,000 native plants, tuatara and scores of birds, including kiwi, kea, moreporks, parakeets and extremely rare black stilts. Stroll around the aviaries, watch the conservation show, and tiptoe quietly into the darkened kiwi houses.

Skyline Gondola CABLE CAR

(☑03-441 0101; www.skyline.co.nz; Brecon St; adult/child return $32/20; ◷9am-late) 🍃 Hop aboard for fantastic views. At the top there's the inevitable cafe, restaurant, souvenir shop and observation deck, as well as the **Queenstown Bike Park** (☑03-441 0101; www.skyline.co.nz; half-/full day incl gondola $60/85; ◷10am-6pm, extended to 8pm as light permits Oct-Apr) Skyline Luge, **Ledge Bungy** (☑0800 286 4958; www.bungy.co.nz; adult/child $195/145), **Ledge Swing** (☑0800 286 4958; www.bungy.co.nz; adult/child $160/110) and **Ziptrek Ecotours** (☑03-441 2102; www.ziptrek.co.nz). At night there are Māori culture shows from Kiwi Haka (p101) and stargazing tours (including gondola adult/child $85/45).

Underwater Observatory VIEWPOINT

(☑03-409 0000; www.kjet.co.nz; main jetty; adult/child $10/5; ◷9am-7pm Nov-Mar, to 5pm Apr-Oct) Six windows showcase life under the lake in this reverse aquarium (the people are

behind glass). Large brown trout abound, and look out for freshwater eels and scaup (diving ducks), which cruise right past the windows – especially when the coin-operated food-release box is triggered.

Activities

Ultimate Hikes
TRAMPING

(☑ 03-450 1940; www.ultimatehikes.co.nz; 9 Duke St; ⊙ Nov-Apr) Offers day walks on the Routeburn Track (from $179) and the Milford Track (from $299), departing from Queenstown. Or you can do these multiday tracks in their entirety, staying in Ultimate Hike's own staffed lodges rather than DOC huts, where hot meals and en suite bathrooms await. In the winter the office is rebranded as Snowbiz and rents skis and snowboards.

Climbing Queenstown
ROCK CLIMBING

(☑ 027 477 9393; www.climbingqueenstown.com; 23 Brecon St; from $149) Rock climbing, via ferrata (climbing with fixed metal rungs, rails, pegs and cables), mountaineering and alpine trekking led by qualified guides.

Shotover Canyon Swing
ADVENTURE SPORTS

(☑ 03-442 6990; www.canyonswing.co.nz; 35 Shotover St; per person $219, additional swings $45) Be released loads of different ways – backwards, in a chair, upside down. From there it's a 60m free fall and a wild swing across the canyon at 150km/h. The price includes the transfer from the Queenstown booking office.

AJ Hackett Bungy
ADVENTURE SPORTS

(☑ 03-450 1300, 0800 286 4958; www.bungy.co.nz; The Station, cnr Camp & Shotover Sts) The bungy originators now offer jumps from three sites in the Queenstown area, with giant swings available at two of them. It all started at the historic 1880 **Kawarau Bridge** (Gibbston Hwy; adult/child $190/145; 23km from Queenstown (transport included). In 1988 it became the world's first commercial bungy site, offering a 43m leap over the river. It's also the only bungy site in the region to offer tandem jumps.

New to the Kawarau Bridge site is the **Kawarau Zipride** (Gibbston Hwy; adult/child $50/40, 3-/5-ride pack $105/150), three 130m ziplines mainly targeted to kids – but also a thrill for adults not keen to take a giant leap of faith. Multi-ride packs can be split between groups, making it a far cheaper alternative to the bungy.

Last but most pant-wetting is the **Nevis Bungy** (per person $275) – the highest bungy in Australasia. 4WD buses will transport you onto private farmland where you can jump from a specially constructed pod, 134m above the Nevis River. The **Nevis Swing** (solo/tandem $195/350) starts 160m above the river and cuts a 300m arc across the canyon on a rope longer than a rugby field – yes, it's the world's biggest swing.

Queenstown Rafting
RAFTING

(☑ 03-442 9792; www.rafting.co.nz; 35 Shotover St; rafting/helirafting $209/309) Rafts year-round on the choppy Shotover River (Grades III to V) and calmer Kawarau River (Grades II to III). Trips take four to five hours with two to three hours on the water. Helirafting trips are an exciting alternative. Participants must be at least 13 years old and weigh more than 40kg.

Shotover Jet
BOAT TOUR

(☑ 03-442 8570; www.shotoverjet.com; Gorge Rd, Arthurs Point; adult/child $135/75) Half-hour jetboat trips through the rocky Shotover Canyon, with lots of thrilling 360-degree spins.

Tours

Million Dollar Cruise
BOAT TOUR

(☑ 03-442 9770; www.milliondollarcruise.co.nz; cruise $35; ⊙ 11am, 2pm & 4pm) Good-value, informative, 90-minute cruises heading up the Frankton end of the lake, past the multi-million-dollar real estate of Kelvin Heights.

ESSENTIAL QUEENSTOWN & WANAKA

Eat A leisurely lunch at a vineyard restaurant.

Drink One of the surprising seasonal brews by Wanaka Beerworks (p102).

Read *Walking the Routeburn Track* by Philip Holden for a wander through the history, flora and fauna of this tramp.

Listen to The silence as you kayak blissfully around Glenorchy and Kinloch.

Watch *Top of the Lake*, the Jane Campion–directed TV series set around the top of Wakatipu.

Online www.queenstownnz.co.nz, www.lakewanaka.co.nz

Area code ☑ 03

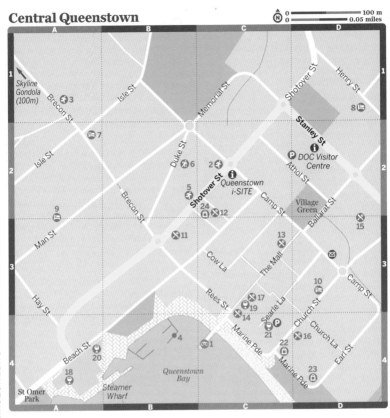

Air Milford SCENIC FLIGHTS

(☑ 03-442 2351; www.airmilford.co.nz; 1 Tex Smith Lane, Frankton) Options include a Milford Sound flyover (adult/child $420/255), a fly-cruise-fly combo ($499/300), and longer flights to Doubtful Sound and Aoraki/Mt Cook.

🛏 Sleeping

Haka Lodge HOSTEL **$**

(☑ 03-442 4970; www.hakalodge.com; 6 Henry St; dm/r without bathroom from $31/89, apt $180; P 🛜) Slap your thighs and kick up your heels, this *haka* is well worth participating in. In response to traveller research, the brightly painted dorms have custom-built bunks including large lockable storage chests, privacy curtains, personal lights and electrical sockets. There's also a two-bedroom apartment attached, with its own kitchen, spacious lounge and laundry facilities.

Nomads HOSTEL **$**

(☑ 03-441 3922; www.nomadsworld.com; 5 Church St; dm with/without bathroom $32/30, r $110-140; @ 🛜) 🖉 With a prime location in the heart of Queenstown's nightlife, this massive hostel has facilities galore, including its own mini-cinema, en suite rooms, large kitchens, a free sauna and an on-site travel agency. It even sweetens the deal with free breakfast and dinner.

YHA Queenstown Lakefront HOSTEL **$**

(☑ 03-442 8413; www.yha.co.nz; 88-90 Lake Esplanade; dm/s/d without bathroom from $32/70/89; @) 🖉 This large lakefront hostel has recently been renovated. Queenstown's nightlife is a 10- to 15-minute lakeside stroll away.

Central Queenstown

◎ Sights
1 Underwater Observatory...................C4

◆ Activities, Courses & Tours
2 AJ Hackett Bungy............................C2
3 Climbing Queenstown.......................A1
4 Million Dollar Cruise B4
5 Queenstown Rafting........................B2
 Shotover Canyon Swing................(see 5)
6 Ultimate Hikes...............................B2

⊜ Sleeping
7 Dairy..A2
8 Haka Lodge....................................D1
9 Lomond Lodge................................A2
10 Nomads..D3

✖ Eating
11 Fergburger....................................B3

12 Habebe's..C2
13 Kappa..C3
14 Madam Woo....................................C4
15 Rata...D3
16 Sasso...D4
17 Winnie's..C3

☼ Drinking & Nightlife
18 Atlas Beer Cafe...............................A4
19 Ballarat Trading
 Company.......................................C3
20 Pub on Wharf.................................A4
21 Zephyr..C4

⊜ Shopping
22 Artbay Gallery.................................C4
23 Vesta..D4
24 Walk In Wardrobe.............................C2

**Creeksyde Queenstown
Holiday Park & Motels**   HOLIDAY PARK $$
(✍03-442 9447; www.camp.co.nz; 54 Robins Rd;
site $55, d without bathroom $81, units from $138;
ⓅＡ🐾） ✎ In a garden setting, this pretty
and extremely well-kept holiday park has ac-
commodation ranging from small tent sites
to fully self-contained motel units. Quirky
touches include oddball sculptures and an
ablutions block disguised as a medieval oast
house (hop kiln).

Coronation Lodge   LODGE $$
(✍03-441 0860; www.coronationlodge.co.nz; 10
Coronation Dr; d $170-210; Ⓟ🐾) Right beside
Queenstown Gardens, this tidy block has
basement parking, plush bed linen, wood-
en floors and Turkish rugs. Larger rooms
have kitchenettes. The attractive little wood-
lined breakfast room at the front serves
both cooked and continental options (costs
extra).

Alexis   MOTEL $$
(✍03-409 0052; www.alexisqueenstown.co.nz; 69
Frankton Rd; unit from $165; Ⓟ🐾) This modern
hillside motel is an easy 10-minute walk
from town along the lakefront. The pleasant
self-contained units have thoughtful extras
such as stereos and robes, along with beaut
lake views.

Lomond Lodge   MOTEL $$
(✍03-442 7375; www.lomondlodge.com; 33 Man
St; d $145-169; Ⓟ🐾) A makeover has mod-
ernised this midrange motel's decor. Share
your on-the-road stories with fellow travellers around the garden barbecue or in the

guest kitchen, although all rooms also have
their own fridges and microwaves. It's worth
paying extra for a lake view.

★Dairy   BOUTIQUE HOTEL $$$
(✍03-442 5164; www.thedairy.co.nz; 10 Isle St; s/d
from $435/465; Ⓟ🐾) Once a corner store, the
Dairy is now a luxury B&B with 13 rooms
packed with classy touches such as designer
bed linen, silk cushions and luxurious mo-
hair rugs. Rates include cooked breakfasts
and freshly baked afternoon teas.

✖ Eating

★Fergbaker   BAKERY $
(42 Shotover St; items $5-9; ⊙6.30am-4.30am)
Fergburger's sweeter sister bakes all man-
ner of tempting treats – and although most
things look tasty with 3am beer goggles on,
it withstands the daylight test admirably.
Goodies include meat pies, filled rolls, Dan-
ish pastries and banoffee tarts. If you're after
gelato, call into Mrs Ferg next door.

Habebe's   MIDDLE EASTERN $
(✍03-442 9861; www.habebes.co.nz; Plaza Arcade,
30 Shotover St; meals $8-18; ⊙8am-5pm; ✎)
Middle Eastern–inspired kebabs, salads and
wraps are the go. Soups and yummy pies
(try the chicken, kumara and mushroom
one) break the mould.

Public Kitchen & Bar   MODERN NZ $$
(✍03-442 5969; www.publickitchen.co.nz; Steam-
er Wharf, Beach St; dishes $15-45; ⊙9am-11pm)
The trend towards informal, shared dining
has come to Queenstown in the form of this

excellent waterfront eatery. Grab a posse and order a selection of plates of varying sizes from the menu; the meaty dishes, in particular, are excellent.

Madam Woo
MALAYSIAN $$

(☑ 03-442 9200; www.madamwoo.co.nz; 5 The Mall; mains $16-32; ☺noon-late; ▣) Wooing customers with a playful take on Chinese and Malay hawker food, the Madame serves up lots of tasty snacks for sharing (wontons, steamed dumplings, greasy filled-roti rolls), alongside larger dishes (beef rendang, duck salad, sambal prawns). Kids and distracted adults alike can have fun colouring in the menu.

Sasso
ITALIAN $$

(☑ 03-409 0994; www.sasso.co.nz; 14 Church St; mains $26-36; ☺4-11pm) Whether you're snuggled by one of the fireplaces inside the stone cottage (1882) or you've landed a table under the summer stars on the front terrace, this upmarket Italian eatery isn't short on atmosphere. Thankfully the food is also excellent.

Winnie's
PIZZA $$

(www.winnies.co.nz; L1, 7 The Mall; mains $18-29; ☺noon-late; ☎) Part-bar and part-restaurant, Winnie's always seems busy. Pizzas with a Thai, Mexican or Moroccan accent and massive burgers, pasta and steaks soak up the alcohol and keep energy levels high. On balmy nights the whole roof opens up and the party continues into the wee smalls.

Kappa
JAPANESE $$

(☑ 03-441 1423; L1, 36a The Mall; lunch $11-17, dinner $16-20; ☺noon-2.30pm & 5.30pm-late Mon-Sat) See if you can grab a spot on the tiny balcony so you can watch the passing parade on the Mall as you down a sake or Japanese beer and graze your way through *izakaya*-style dishes (food to snack on while you're drinking). The menu is short, sharp and very tasty.

Rata
MODERN NZ $$$

(☑ 03-442 9393; www.ratadining.co.nz; 43 Ballarat St; mains $36-42, 2-/3-course lunch $28/38; ☺noon-11pm) After gaining Michelin stars for restaurants in London, New York and LA, chef-owner Josh Emett has brought his exceptional but surprisingly unflashy cooking back home in the form of this upmarket but informal back-lane eatery. Native bush, edging the windows and in a large-scale photographic mural, sets the scene for a short menu showcasing the best seasonal NZ produce.

🍷 Drinking & Nightlife

Zephyr
BAR

(☑ 03-409 0852; www.facebook.com/zephyrqt; 1 Searle Lane; ☺8pm-4am) Queenstown's coolest indie rock bar is located – as all such places should be – in a grungy basement off a back

Queenstown waterfront dining

QUEENSTOWN & WANAKA QUEENSTOWN

lane. There's a popular pool table and regular live bands.

Atlas Beer Cafe
BAR

(☑ 03-442 5995; www.atlasbeercafe.com; Steamer Wharf, Beach St; ☺ 10am-late) Perched at the end of Steamer Wharf, this pint-sized bar specialises in beers from Dunedin's Emerson's Brewery and Queenstown's Altitude and regular guest brews from further afield. It's also one of the best places in Queenstown for a good-value meal, serving excellent cooked breakfasts and simple hearty fare such as steaks, burgers and chicken parmigiana (mains $10 to $20).

Ballarat Trading Company
PUB

(☑ 03-442 4222; www.ballarat.co.nz; 7-9 The Mall; ☺ 11am-4am) Beyond the eclectic decor (stuffed bear, rampant wall-mounted ducks), Ballarat is quite a traditional spot, with gleaming beer taps, cover bands, sports on TV, quiz nights, occasional lapses into 1980s music and robust meals.

Pub on Wharf
PUB

(☑ 03-441 2155; www.pubonwharf.co.nz; 88 Beach St; ☺ 10am-late; ☎) Ubercool interior design combines with handsome woodwork and lighting fit for a hipster hideaway, with fake sheep heads to remind you that you're still in NZ. Mac's beers on tap, scrummy nibbles and a decent wine list make this a great place to settle in for the evening. There's live music nightly and comedy occasionally.

☆ Entertainment

Sherwood
LIVE MUSIC

(☑ 03-450 1090; www.sherwoodqueenstown.nz; 554 Frankton Rd, Queenstown East) As well as being a brilliant spot for a meal or a drink, the Sherwood has quickly become Queenstown's go-to spot for visiting musos. Many of NZ's bigger names have performed here; check the website for coming gigs.

Kiwi Haka
TRADITIONAL MUSIC

(☑ 03-441 0101; www.skyline.co.nz; Skyline; adult/child excl gondola $39/26) For a traditional Māori cultural experience, head to the top of the gondola for one of the 30-minute shows. There are usually three shows per night; bookings are essential.

🛍 Shopping

★ Vesta
ARTS, CRAFTS

(☑ 03-442 5687; www.vestadesign.co.nz; 19 Marine Pde; ☺ 10am-6pm) Showcasing really cool NZ-made art and craft, Vesta is full of interesting prints, paintings, glass art and gifts. It's housed in Williams Cottage (1864), Queenstown's oldest home. It's worth visiting just to check out the 1930s wallpaper and 1920s garden.

Artbay Gallery
ARTS

(☑ 03-442 9090; www.artbay.co.nz; 13 Marine Pde; ☺ 11am-6pm Mon-Wed, to 9pm Thu-Sun) Occupying an attractive 1863-built Freemason's Hall on the lakefront, Artbay is always an interesting place to peruse, even if you don't have thousands to spend on a delicately carved ram's skull. It showcases the work of contemporary NZ artists, most of whom have a connection to the region.

Walk In Wardrobe
CLOTHING

(☑ 03-409 0190; www.thewalkinwardrobe.co.nz; Beech Tree Arcade, 34 Shotover St; ☺ 10am-6pm Tue & Wed, to 8.30pm Thu-Mon) Benefiting from wealthy travellers lightening their suitcases before jetting out, this 'preloved fashion boutique' is a great place to hunt for bargain designer duds. Womenswear fills most of the racks.

ℹ Information

DOC Visitor Centre (☑ 03-442 7935; www.doc.govt.nz; 50 Stanley St; ☺ 8.30am-5pm) Head here to pick up confirmed bookings for the Routeburn Track and backcountry hut passes, and to get the latest weather and track updates. It can also advise on walks to suit your level of ability.

Post Office (☑ 0800 501 501; www.nzpost.co.nz; 13 Camp St; ☺ 9am-5pm Mon-Fri, 10am-2pm Sat)

Queenstown i-SITE (☑ 03-442 4100; www.queenstowninformation.com; cnr Shotover & Camp Sts; ☺ 8.30am-7pm) Friendly and informative despite being perpetually frantic, the saintly staff here can help with bookings and information on Queenstown, Gibbston, Lake Hayes, Arrowtown and Glenorchy.

Wanaka

◎ Sights

National Transport & Toy Museum
MUSEUM

(☑ 03-443 8765; www.nttmuseumwanaka.co.nz; 891 Wanaka Luggate Hwy/SH6; adult/child $17/5; ☺ 8.30am-5pm; ⊞) Small armies of Smurfs, Star Wars figurines and Barbie dolls share billing with dozens of classic cars and a mysteriously acquired MiG jet fighter in

this vast collection, which fills four giant hangars near the airport. There are around 30,000 items in total, including plenty of toys that you're bound to remember from rainy childhood afternoons.

Puzzling World
AMUSEMENT PARK
(☑03-443 7489; www.puzzlingworld.com; 188 Wanaka Luggate Hwy/SH84; adult/child $20/14; ⏰8.30am-5.30pm; ⊞) A 3D Great Maze and lots of fascinating brain-bending visual illusions to keep people of all ages bemused, bothered and bewildered. It's en route to Cromwell, 2km from town.

Rippon
WINERY
(☑03-443 8084; www.rippon.co.nz; 246 Mt Aspiring Rd; ⏰noon-5pm Jul-Apr) Along with just about the best view of any NZ winery, Rippon has great wine, too. To save fights over who's going to be the designated driver, take a 2km stroll along the lakeside and look out for the track up the hill from the end of Sargood Dr.

Wanaka Beerworks
BREWERY
(☑03-443 1865; www.wanakabeerworks.co.nz; 891 Wanaka Luggate Hwy/SH6; tours incl tasting $15; ⏰tours 2pm Sun-Thu) Somewhat incongruously attached to the toy museum, this small brewery's main beers (Cardrona Gold lager, Brewski pilsner, Treble Cone wheat beer and Black Peak coffee stout) are complemented by those of its sister label Jabberwocky, along with various seasonal brews.

🏃 Activities

Aspiring Guides
ADVENTURE SPORTS
(☑03-443 9422; www.aspiringguides.com; L1, 99 Ardmore St) This crew offers a multitude of options, including guided wilderness tramping (from two to eight days); mountaineering and ice-climbing courses; guided ascents of Tititea/Mt Aspiring, Aoraki/Mt Cook, Mt Brewster and Mt Tasman; and off-piste skiing (one- to five-day backcountry expeditions).

Basecamp Wanaka
ROCK CLIMBING
(☑03-443 1110; www.basecampwanaka.co.nz; 50 Cardrona Valley Rd; day pass $23-30; ⏰noon-8pm Mon-Fri, 10am-6pm Sat & Sun) Before you hit the mountains, learn the ropes on climbing walls. Even fearless three-year-olds can have a go on the Clip 'n Climb (from $10).

Wanaka Rock Climbing
ROCK CLIMBING
(☑03-443 6411; www.wanakarock.co.nz) Introductory rock-climbing course (half-/full day

$140/210), a half-day abseiling intro ($140), and bouldering and multipitch climbs for the experienced.

Good Rotations
BICYCLE RENTAL
(☑027 874 7377; www.goodrotations.co; 34 Anderson Rd; half-/full day $59/89) Hires bicycles including electric bikes and all-terrain 'fat bikes' with superwide tyres (great for the pebbles on the lakefront). Drop by the neighbouring coffee-and-food cart for a pre-ride rev-up.

👉 Tours

U-Fly
SCENIC FLIGHTS
(☑03-445 4005; www.u-flywanaka.co.nz; from $199) Scratch 'flying a plane' off the bucket list on a scenic flight over Mt Aspiring National Park. Don't fret: there are dual controls ready for the pilots to take over at a moment's notice – they're not completely insane.

Wanaka Bike Tours
MOUNTAIN BIKING
(☑03-443 6363; www.wanakabiketours.co.nz; from $199) Guided trips including helibiking options.

Eco Wanaka Adventures
TRAMPING, CRUISE
(☑03-443 2869; www.ecowanaka.co.nz) 🚶 Guided tours include a full-day trek to the Rob Roy Glacier ($275), a four-hour cruise and walk on Mou Waho island ($225), and a full-day cruise-4WD combo ($450). Also offers helihikes.

Wanaka River Journeys
TOUR
(☑03-443 4416; www.wanakariverjourneys.co.nz; adult/child $229/139) 🚶 Combination bush walk (50 minutes) and jetboat ride in the gorgeous Matukituki Valley.

🛏 Sleeping

⭐ Wanaka Bakpaka
HOSTEL $
(☑03-443 7837; www.wanakabakpaka.co.nz; 117 Lakeside Rd; dm $30-31, d with/without bathroom $92/74; @🛜) An energetic husband-and-wife team run this friendly hostel above the lake with just about the best views in town. Amenities are top-shelf and the onto-it staff consistently offer a red-carpet welcome to weary travellers. It's worth considering paying a bit extra for the en suite double with the gorgeous views.

YHA Wanaka Purple Cow
HOSTEL $
(☑03-443 1880; www.yha.co.nz; 94 Brownston St; dm $30-35, d with/without bathroom from $100/89; @🛜) 🚶 In the top echelons of

Wanaka

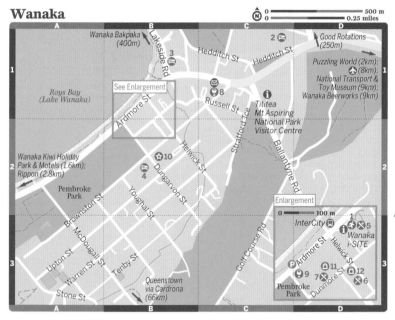

Wanaka

🟢 Activities, Courses & Tours
1 Aspiring Guides D3

🔵 Sleeping
2 Criffel Peak View C1
3 Lakeside B1
4 YHA Wanaka Purple Cow B2

⚫ Eating
5 Francesca's Italian Kitchen D3
6 Spice Room D3
7 Yohei D3

🟢 Drinking & Nightlife
8 Barluga & Woody's C1
9 Gin & Raspberry D3
Lalaland .... (see 1)

🟢 Entertainment
10 Cinema Paradiso B2

🔴 Shopping
11 Chop Shop D3
12 Gallery Thirty Three D3

NZ YHAs, the Purple Cow offers a range of shared and private rooms, including some with en suites in a newer building out the back. Best of all is the large lounge, with commanding lake and mountain views and a wood stove.

**Wanaka Kiwi
Holiday Park & Motels** HOLIDAY PARK $
(☑ 03-443 7766; www.wanakakiwiholidaypark. nz; 263 Studholme Rd North; campsites $25-27, units with/without bathroom from $100/85; @ ☎) Grassy sites for tents and campervans, lots of trees, and pretty views add up to a charming and relaxing campground. Facilities include a barbecue area with gas heaters, and

free wi-fi, spa pool and sauna. Older-style motel units have all been renovated, and the newest budget cabins are warm and cosy with wooden floors.

⭐ **Alpine View Lodge** B&B $$
(☑ 03-443 7111; www.alpineviewlodge.co.nz; 23 Studholme Rd South; d from $180, cottage $285; ☎) In a peaceful, rural setting on the edge of town, this excellent lodge has three B&B rooms, one of which has its own, private, bush-lined deck. Little extras include home-made shortbread in the rooms and a hot tub. Alternatively, you can opt for the fully self-contained two-bedroom cottage, which opens onto the garden.

★Criffel Peak View B&B $$

(☑03-443 5511; www.criffelpeakview.co.nz; 98 Hedditch St; s/d/apt from $135/160/270; 🛜) Situated in a quiet cul-de-sac, this excellent B&B has three rooms sharing a large lounge with a log fire and a sunny wisteria-draped deck. The charming hostesses live in a separate house behind, which also has a self-contained two-bedroom apartment attached.

★Lakeside APARTMENTS $$$

(☑03-443 0188; www.lakesidewanaka.co.nz; 7 Lakeside Rd; apt from $295; 🛜📶) 🍴 Luxuriate in a modern apartment in a prime position overlooking the lake, by the town centre. All have three bedrooms but can be rented with only one or two bedrooms open. The swimming pool is a rarity in these parts and an appealing alternative to the frigid lake on a sweltering day.

✗ Eating

Florence's Foodstore & Cafe CAFE $

(☑03-443 7078; www.florencesfoodstore.co.nz; 71 Cardrona Valley Rd; mains $9.50-18; ⊙8.30am-3pm) Wood, corrugated iron and jute-cladding create a rustic feel for this edge-of-town gourmet provedore. Call in for the region's prettiest smoked salmon benedict, as well as Frenchstyle pastries and delicious filled bagels.

Yohei JAPANESE $

(☑03-443 4222; Spencer House Mall, 23 Dunmore St; mains $9-14; ⊙9am-5.30pm; 🛜🍴) Tucked away in a shopping arcade, this relaxed eatery does interesting local spins on sushi (how about venison?), Japanese curries, noodles and superlative juices and smoothies.

★Francesca's Italian Kitchen ITALIAN $$

(☑03-443 5599; www.fransitalian.co.nz; 93 Ardmore St; mains $20-26; ⊙noon-3pm & 5pm-late) Ebullient expat Francesca has brought the big flavours and easy conviviality of an authentic Italian family trattoria to Wanaka in the form of this stylish and perennially busy eatery. Even simple things such as pizza, pasta and polenta chips are exceptional. She also runs a pizza cart on Brownston St, opposite Cinema Paradiso.

Spice Room INDIAN $$

(☑03-443 1133; www.spiceroom.co.nz; 43 Helwick St; mains $21-27; ⊙5-10pm; 🍴) The combination of authentic curry, crispy garlic naan and cold beer is a great way to recharge after a day's snowboarding or tramping. Beyond the spot-on renditions of all your subcontinental favourites, the Spice Room springs a few surprises, with starters including a zingy scallop masala salad.

🍺 Drinking & Nightlife

Gin & Raspberry COCKTAIL BAR

(☑03-443 4216; www.ginandraspberry.co.nz; L1, 155 Ardmore St; ⊙3pm-late) If you're in the swing for bling, this lush bar offers gilded mirrors, sparkling chandeliers, a piano and a central fireplace. Classic movies provide a backdrop to classic cocktails (including various martinis), and the occasional live band fires things up.

Lalaland COCKTAIL BAR

(☑03-443 4911; www.lalalandwanaka.co.nz; L1, 99 Ardmore St; ⊙6pm-2.30am) Keep a watchful eye on the lake or sink into a comfy chair at this little, low-lit, completely over-the-top cocktail palace/bordello. The young barmeister-owner truly knows his stuff, concocting elixirs to suit every mood. Entry is via the rear stairs.

Barluga & Woody's BAR

(☑03-443 5400; Post Office Lane, 33 Ardmore St; ⊙4pm-2.30am) Sharing both a courtyard and owners, these neighbouring bars operate more or less in tandem, especially when there's a DJ event on. Barluga's leather armchairs and retro wallpaper bring to mind a refined gentlemen's club. Wicked cocktails and killer back-to-back beats soon smash that illusion. Woody's plays the role of the younger, sportier brother, with pool tables and indie sounds.

☆ Entertainment

Ruby's CINEMA

(☑03-443 6901; www.rubyscinema.co.nz; 50 Cardrona Valley Rd; adult/child $19/15) Channelling a lush New York or Shanghai vibe, this hip-art-house-cinema-meets-chic-cocktail-bar is a real surprise in outdoorsy Wanaka. Luxuriate in the huge cinema seats, or chill out in the red-velvet lounge with craft beers, classic cocktails and sophisticated bar snacks. You'll find Ruby's concealed within the Basecamp Wanaka building on the outskirts of town.

Cinema Paradiso CINEMA

(☑03-443 1505; www.paradiso.net.nz; 72 Brownston St; adult/child $15/9.50) Stretch out on a comfy couch, a dentist's chair or in an old Morris Minor at this Wanaka institution, screening the best of Hollywood and

Lake Wanaka

art-house flicks. At intermission the smell of freshly baked cookies and pizza wafts through the theatre, although the home-made ice cream is just as alluring.

Shopping

Chop Shop CLOTHING
(☑ 03-443 8297; www.chopshopwanaka.co.nz; 3 Pembroke Mall; ⊘10am-6pm) The best coffee in town and a natty range of locally designed beanies and cool T-shirts for the discerning snowboarder.

Gallery Thirty Three ARTS, CRAFTS
(☑ 03-443 4330; www.gallery33.co.nz; 33 Helwick St; ⊘10am-5pm) Pottery, glass and jewellery from local artists.

ⓘ Information

Tititea Mt Aspiring National Park Visitor Centre (☑ 03-443 7660; www.doc.govt.nz; cnr Ardmore & Ballantyne Sts; ⊘8.30am-5pm daily Nov-Apr, Mon-Sat May-Oct) In an A-frame building on the edge of the town centre, this DOC centre takes hut bookings and offers advice on tracks and conditions. Be sure to call in before undertaking any wilderness tramps. There's also a small display on Wanaka geology, flora and fauna.

Wanaka i-SITE (☑ 03-443 1233; www.lake-wanaka.co.nz; 103 Ardmore St; ⊘8.30am-5.30pm) Extremely helpful but always busy.

Wanaka Medical Centre (☑ 03-443 0710; www.wanakamedical.co.nz; 23 Cardrona Valley Rd; ⊘9am-5pm Mon-Fri) Patches up adventure-sports mishaps.

Makarora

🏃 Activities

The best short walk in this secluded area is the **Haast Pass Lookout Track** (one hour return, 3.5km), which offers great views from above the bush line. Other options include the **Bridle Track** (1½ hours one way, 3.5km), from the top of Haast Pass to Davis Flat, and the **Blue Pools Walk** (30 minutes return), where you may see huge rainbow and brown trout.

Longer tramps go through magnificent countryside but shouldn't be undertaken lightly. Changeable alpine and river conditions mean you must be well prepared; consult with DOC before heading off. Its *Tramping in the Makarora Region* brochure ($2) is a worthwhile investment. Call into the Tititea Mt Aspiring National Park Visitor Centre in Wanaka to check conditions and routes before undertaking any wilderness tramps.

Gillespie Pass TRAMPING
The three-day Gillespie Pass loop tramp goes via the Young, Siberia and Wilkin Valleys. This is a high pass with avalanche danger in winter and spring. With a jetboat ride down the Wilkin to complete it, it rates as one of NZ's most memorable tramps. Jetboats go to Kerin Forks, and a service goes across

the Young River mouth when the Makarora floods.

Wilkin Valley Track TRAMPING
The Wilkin Valley Track starts from the Makarora River and heads along the Wilkin River to the Kerin Forks Hut (four to five hours, 15km). After another day's walk up the valley you'll reach the Top Forks Huts (six to eight hours, 15km), from which the picturesque Lakes Diana, Lucidus and Castalia (one hour, 1½ hours, and three to four hours respectively) can be reached.

Wilkin River Jets BOATING
(☑03-443 8351; www.wilkinriverjets.co.nz; adult/child $119/69) A superb 50km, one-hour jet-boating trip into Mt Aspiring National Park, following the Makarora and Wilkin Rivers. Trips can be combined with a helicopter ride.

👉 Tours

Siberia Experience ADVENTURE TOUR
See p43

Southern Alps Air SCENIC FLIGHTS
(☑03-443 4385, 0800 345 666; www.southernalpsair.co.nz) 🗲 Flies to Aoraki/Mt Cook and the glaciers (adult/child $445/285), along with Milford Sound flyovers ($415/265) and Milford fly-cruise combos ($498/315).

❶ Information

Makarora Tourist Centre (☑03-443 8372; www.makarora.co.nz; 5944 Haast Pass-

Makarora Rd/SH6; ⊙8am-8pm) A large complex incorporating a cafe, bar, shop, information centre, campground, bunk house and self-contained units.

Cromwell

⊙ Sights

Cromwell Heritage Precinct HISTORIC BUILDINGS
(www.cromwellheritageprecinct.co.nz; Melmore Tce) When the Clyde Dam was completed in 1992 it flooded Cromwell's historic town centre, 280 homes, six farms and 17 orchards. Many historic buildings were disassembled before the flooding and have since been rebuilt in a pedestrianised precinct beside Lake Dunstan. While some have been set up as period pieces (stables and the like), others house some good cafes, galleries and interesting shops.

🏃 Activities

Highlands Motorsport Park ADVENTURE SPORTS
(☑03-445 4052; www.highlands.co.nz; cnr SH6 & Sandflat Rd; ⊙10am-5pm) Transformed from a paddock into a top-notch 4km racing circuit in just 18 months, this rev-heads' paradise hosted its first major event in 2013. The action isn't reserved just for the professionals, with various high-octane experiences on offer, along with an excellent museum.

MICAH WRIGHT/GETTY IMAGES ©

Jetboating along Wilkin River

Tours

Central Otago Motorcycle Hire   TOUR
(✆03-445 4487; www.comotorcyclehire.co.nz; 271 Bannockburn Rd; per day from $165) The sinuous and hilly roads of Central Otago are perfect for negotiating on two wheels. This crew hires out bikes and advises on improbably scenic routes. It also offers guided trail-bike tours (from $195) and extended road tours (from $575).

Goldfields Jet   ADVENTURE TOUR
(✆03-445 1038; www.goldfieldsjet.co.nz; SH6; adult/child $109/49) Zip through the Kawarau Gorge on a 40-minute jetboat ride.

Festivals & Events

Highlands 101   SPORTS
(☉Nov) A three-day motor-racing festival at Highlands Park, including the final round of the Australian GT Championship.

Sleeping

Cromwell Top 10 Holiday Park   HOLIDAY PARK $
(✆03-445 0164; www.cromwellholidaypark.co.nz; 1 Alpha St; sites $40-44, units with/without bathroom from $110/75; @🛜) The size of a small European nation and packed with cabins and self-contained units of various descriptions, all set in tree-lined grounds.

Carrick Lodge   MOTEL $$
(✆03-445 4519; www.carricklodge.co.nz; 10 Barry Ave; units $140-180; 🛜) One of Cromwell's more stylish motels, Carrick has spacious, modern units and is just a short stroll from the main shopping complex. Executive units have spa baths and views over the golf course.

★**Burn Cottage Retreat**   B&B, COTTAGE $$$
(✆03-445 3050; www.burncottageretreat.co.nz; 168 Burn Cottage Rd; r/cottages $200/225; 🛜) Set among walnut trees and gardens 3km

northwest of Cromwell, this peaceful retreat has three luxurious, self-contained cottages with classy decor, spacious kitchens and modern bathrooms. B&B accommodation is available in the main house.

Eating

★**Armando's Kitchen**   CAFE $$
(✆03-445 0303; 71 Melmore Tce; mains $10-22; ☉10am-3pm Sat-Thu, to 9pm Fri, extended hours in summer) Cromwell's heritage precinct is best enjoyed from the veranda of Armando's Kitchen, with an espresso or gourmet ice cream in hand. The homemade pasta, pizza and cakes are all excellent, and the breakfasts are legendary. On Friday nights it opens late for pizza and drinks.

Mt Difficulty   MODERN NZ $$
(✆03-445 3445; www.mtdifficulty.co.nz; 73 Felton Rd, Bannockburn; mains $30-35; ☉tastings 10.30am-4.30pm, restaurant noon-4pm) As well as making our favourite NZ pinot noir, Mt Difficulty is a lovely spot for a leisurely lunch looking down over the valley. There are large wine-friendly platters to share, but save room for the decadent desserts.

Bannockburn Hotel   PUB FOOD $$
(✆03-445 0615; www.bannockburnhotel.com; 420 Bannockburn Rd, Bannockburn; mains $24-30; ☉11am-9pm) Head out to the historic Bannockburn watering hole for massive serves of pub grub (ribs, steaks, fish and chips) and even bigger skies from the front terrace. It's 5km out of town, but it operates a free courtesy bus.

Information

Cromwell i-SITE (✆03-445 0212; www.central otagonz.com; 2d The Mall; ☉9am-7pm Jan-Mar, to 5pm Apr-Dec) Stocks the *Walk Cromwell* brochure, covering local mountain-bike and walking trails, including the nearby gold-rush ghost-town of Bendigo.

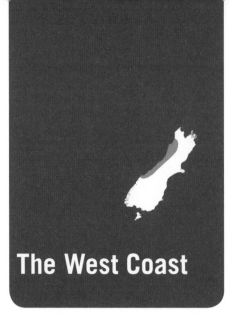

Hemmed in by the wild Tasman Sea and the Southern Alps, the West Coast is like nowhere else in New Zealand.

The West Coast

Hokitika

Sights

★ **Hokitika Museum**   MUSEUM
(www.hokitikamuseum.co.nz; 17 Hamilton St; adult/
child $6/3; ☺10am-5pm Nov-Mar, 10am-2pm
Apr-Oct) Housed in the imposing Carnegie
Building (1908), this is an exemplary provincial museum, with intelligently curated
exhibitions presented in a clear, modern
style. Highlights include the fascinating
Whitebait! exhibition, and the Pounamu
room – the ideal primer before you hit the
galleries looking for greenstone treasures.

★ **Lake Kaniere**   LAKE
(www.doc.govt.nz) Lying at the heart of a
7000-hectare scenic reserve, beautiful Lake
Kaniere is 8km long, 2km wide, 195m deep,
and freezing cold as you'll discover if you
swim. You may, however, prefer simply to
camp or picnic at Hans Bay, or undertake
one of numerous walks in the surrounds,
ranging from the 15-minute Canoe Cove
Walk to the seven-hour return gut-buster
up Mt Tuhua. The historic **Kaniere Water
Race Walkway** (3½ hours one way) forms
part of the West Coast Wilderness Trail.

Hokitika Gorge   GORGE
(www.doc.govt.nz) A picturesque 35km drive
leads to Hokitika Gorge, a ravishing ravine

with unbelievably turquoise waters coloured
by glacial 'flour'. Photograph the scene from
every angle via the short forest walkway and
swingbridge. The gorge is well signposted
from Stafford St (past the dairy factory). En
route, you will pass **Kowhitirangi**, the site of
one of NZ's deadliest mass murders (immor-
talised in the 1982 classic film *Bad Blood*).
A poignant roadside monument lines up the
farmstead site through a stone shaft.

Glowworm Dell   NATURAL FEATURE
On the northern edge of town, a short stroll
from SH6 leads to this glowworm dell, an
easy opportunity to enter the other-worldly
home of NZ's native fungus gnat larvae (so
not even a worm at all). An information
panel at the entrance will further illuminate
your way.

🏃 Activities

Hokitika Heritage Walk   WALKING
Ask staff at the i-SITE for the worthy 50c
leaflet before wandering the old wharf
precinct, or ask them about a guided walk
with Mr Verrall. Another map details the
Hokitika Heritage Trail, an 11km (two- to
three-hour) loop taking in historic sites and
interesting town views.

Wilderness Wings   SCENIC FLIGHTS
(☎0800 755 8118; www.wildernesswings.co.nz;
Hokitika Airport; flights from $285) A highly

Hokitika

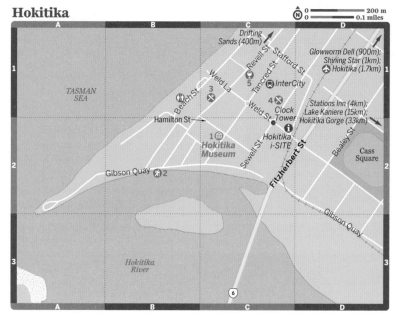

regarded operator running scenic flights over Hokitika and further afield to Aoraki/Mt Cook and the glaciers.

🛏 Sleeping

★ **Drifting Sands**   HOSTEL **$**
(📞 03-755 7654; www.driftingsands.co.nz; 197 Revell St; dm $36, d & tr $109; 🛜) If only all hostels were this stylish. Natural tones and textures, upcycled furniture, chic furnishings and hip vibes make this beachside pad a winner, as does quality bedding, a cosy lounge and hot bread in the morning. Fab!

Hans Bay DOC Campground   CAMPGROUND **$**
(www.doc.govt.nz; sites per adult/child $6/3) This basic DOC campsite occupies a prime spot on grassy terraces with grandstand views of the lake and bushy surrounding hills.

Shining Star   HOLIDAY PARK, MOTEL **$$**
(📞 03-755 8921; 16 Richards Dr; sites unpowered/powered $32/40, d $115-199; 🛜) Attractive and versatile beachside spot with everything from camping to classy self-contained seafront units. Kids will love the menagerie, including pigs and alpacas straight from Dr Doolittle's appointment book. Parents might prefer the spa or sauna.

Hokitika

◎ **Top Sights**
   1 Hokitika Museum C2

⊕ **Activities, Courses & Tours**
   2 Hokitika Heritage Walk B2

⊗ **Eating**
   3 Fat Pipi Pizza C1
   4 Ramble + Ritual C1

⊜ **Drinking & Nightlife**
   5 West Coast Wine Bar C1

Stations Inn   MOTEL **$$**
(📞 03-755 5499; www.stationsinnhokitika.co.nz; Blue Spur Rd; d $170-300; 🛜) Five minutes' drive from town on rolling hills overlooking the distant ocean, this smart, modern motel complex has plush units featuring king-sized beds and spa bath. With a patio, pond and waterwheel out the front, the on-site restaurant (mains $30 to $45; open from 5pm Tuesday to Saturday) specialises in meaty fare.

🍴 Eating & Drinking

Ramble + Ritual   CAFE **$**
(📞 03-755 6347; 51 Sewell St; snacks $3-8, meals $8-15; ⊗ 8am-4pm Mon-Fri, 9am-1pm Sat; 🍴)

109

Tucked away near the Clock Tower, this gallery-cum-cafe is a stylish little spot to linger over great espresso, delicious fresh baking and simple, healthy salads made to order. The ginger oaty may well be the best in the land.

★**Fat Pipi Pizza**   PIZZA **$$**
(89 Revell St; pizzas $20-30; ⊙noon-2.30pm Wed-Sun, 5-9pm daily; ✐) Vegetarians, carnivores and everyone in between will be salivating for the pizza (including a whitebait version) made with love right before your eyes. Lovely cakes, honey buns and Benger juices, too. Best enjoyed in the garden bar – one of the West Coast's best dining spots.

West Coast Wine Bar   WINE BAR
(www.westcoastwine.co.nz; 108 Revell St; ⊙8am-late Tue-Sat, 8am-2pm Mon) Upping Hoki's sophistication factor, this weeny joint with a cute garden bar packs a fridge full of fine wine and craft beer, with the option of ordering up pizza from Fat Pipi Pizza, down the road.

❶ Information

Hokitika i-SITE (✐03-755 6166; www.hokitika.org; 36 Weld St; ⊙8.30am-6pm Mon-Fri, 9am-5pm Sat & Sun) One of NZ's best i-SITEs offers extensive bookings, including all bus services. Also holds DOC info, although you'll need to

book online or at DOC visitor centres further afield. See also www.westcoastnz.com.

Westland Medical Centre (✐03-755 8180; 54a Sewell St; ⊙8am-4.45pm Mon-Fri) Ring after hours.

Fox Glacier

◉ Sights & Activities

Fox Glacier Lookout   LOOKOUT
This is one of the best land-based positions from which to see Fox Glacier, although its retreat may mean you see just a snippet.

★**Lake Matheson**   TRAMPING
(www.doc.govt.nz) The famous 'mirror lake' can be found about 6km down Cook Flat Rd. Wandering slowly (as you should), it will take 1½ hours to complete the circuit. The best time to visit is early morning, or when the sun is low in the late afternoon, although the presence of the Matheson Cafe (p112) means that any time is a good time.

Fox Glacier Guiding   GUIDED WALK
(✐03-751 0825, 0800 111 600; www.foxguides.co.nz; 44 Main Rd) Guided helihikes (equipment provided) are organised by Fox Glacier Guiding. The standard trip (up to three hours on the ice) is $399/369 per adult/child, but there are other options, including an easy-going two-hour interpretive walk to the glacier (adult/child $59/45). Note that age restrictions vary depending on the trip.

Skydive Fox Glacier   SKYDIVING
(✐0800 751 0080, 03-751 0080; www.skydivefox.co.nz; Fox Glacier Airfield, SH6) Eye-popping scenery abounds on leaps from 16,500ft ($399) or 13,000ft ($299). The airfield is conveniently located three minutes' walk from the village centre.

Fox & Franz Josef Heliservices SCENIC FLIGHTS
(✐03-751 0866, 0800 800 793; www.scenic-flights.co.nz; 44 Main Rd; 20-40min flights $210-420) Operator with over 30 years' experience zipping sightseers up and down the glaciers, and around Aoraki/Mt Cook on longer flights. It also has an office in Franz Josef.

🛏 Sleeping

★**Fox Glacier**
Top 10 Holiday Park   HOLIDAY PARK **$**
(✐0800 154 366, 03-751 0821; www.fghp.co.nz; Kerrs Rd; sites $42-45, cabins & units $73-255; @❡) This park has options to suit all budg-

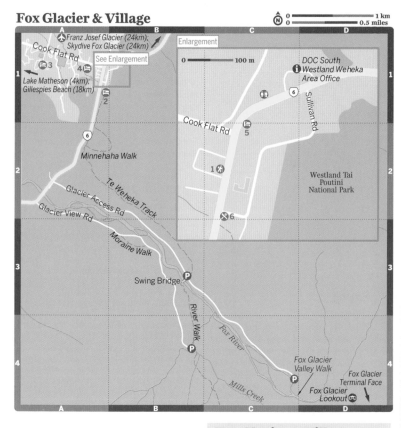

ets, from grassy and hard campervan sites to lodge rooms and upscale motel units. Excellent amenities include a modern communal kitchen and dining room, playground and spa pool, but it's the mountain views that give it the X-factor.

Westhaven   MOTEL **$$**

(☑0800 369 452, 03-751 0084; www.thewesthaven.co.nz; SH6; d $145-185; ☎) These smart suites are a classy combo of corrugated steel and local stone amid burnt-red and ivory walls. The deluxe king rooms have spa baths, and there are bikes to hire for the energetic (half-/full day $20/40).

Rainforest Motel   MOTEL **$$**

(☑0800 724 636, 03-751 0140; www.rainforestmotel.co.nz; 15 Cook Flat Rd; d $125-160; ☎) Rustic log cabins on the outside with neutral decor on the inside. Epic lawns for running around on or simply enjoying the mountain views. A tidy, good-value option.

Fox Glacier & Village

◑ Activities, Courses & Tours

Fox & Franz Josef
    Heliservices .... (see 1)
1 Fox Glacier Guiding.............................. C2

◖ Sleeping

2 Fox Glacier Lodge................................ A1
3 Fox Glacier Top 10 Holiday Park......... A1
4 Rainforest Motel A1
5 Westhaven.. C2

◗ Eating

6 Last Kitchen... C2

Fox Glacier Lodge   B&B, MOTEL **$$$**

(☑0800 369 800, 03-751 0888; www.foxglacierlodge.com; 41 Sullivan Rd; d $175-225; ☎) Beautiful timber adorns the exterior and interior of this attractive property, imparting a mountain-chalet vibe. Similarly woody self-contained mezzanine units with spa baths and gas fires are also available.

Ice cave, Fox Glacier
MICHAEL RUNKEL/GETTY IMAGES ©

 Eating

★**Matheson Cafe** MODERN NZ **$$**

(☑03-751 0878; www.lakematheson.com; Lake Matheson Rd; breakfast & lunch $10-21, dinner $17-33; ☺8am-late Nov-Mar, to 4pm Apr-Oct) Next to Lake Matheson, this cafe does everything right: sharp architecture that maximises inspiring mountain views, strong coffee, craft beers and upmarket fare from a smoked-salmon breakfast bagel, to slow-cooked lamb followed by berry crumble. Part of the complex is the ReflectioNZ Gallery next door, stocking quality, primarily NZ-made art and souvenirs.

Last Kitchen CAFE **$$**

(☑03-751 0058; cnr Sullivan Rd & SH6; lunch $10-20, dinner $24-32; ☺11.30am-late) Making the most of its sunny corner location with outside tables, the Last Kitchen is a good option, serving contemporary fare, such as haloumi salad, pistachio-crusted lamb and genuinely gourmet burgers. It also satisfies for coffee and a wine later in the day.

❶ Information

Activity operators and accommodation providers are well-oiled at providing information on local services (and usually a booking service, too), but you can also find info online at www.glaciercountry.co.nz. Note that there's no ATM in Fox (which means no cash out south until Wanaka), and that **Fox Glacier Motors** (☑03-751 0823; SH6) is your last chance for fuel before Haast, 120km away.

DOC South Westland Weheka Area Office (☑03-751 0807; SH6; ☺10am-2pm Mon-Fri) This is no longer a general visitor-information centre, but has the usual DOC information, hut tickets, and weather and track updates.

Fox Glacier Health Centre (☑0800 7943 2584, 03-751 0836; SH6) Clinic opening hours are displayed at the centre, or ring the ☑0800 number for assistance from the Franz Josef Health Centre.

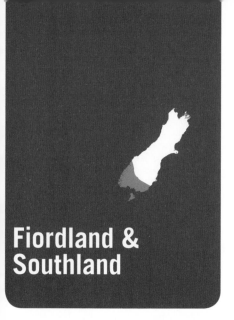

Fiordland & Southland

Welcome to scenery that travellers dream of and cameras fail to do justice to.

Te Anau

◉ Sights

Punanga Manu o Te Anau　　BIRD SANCTUARY
(www.doc.govt.nz; Te Anau–Manapouri Rd; ☉dawn-dusk) FREE By the lake, this set of outdoor aviaries offers a chance to see native bird species difficult to spot in the wild, including the precious icon of Fiordland, the extremely rare takahe.

Te Anau Glowworm Caves　　CAVE
(☑0800 656 501; www.realjourneys.co.nz; adult/child $79/22) Once present only in Māori legends, these impressive caves were rediscovered in 1948. Accessible only by boat, the 200m-long system of caves is a magical place with sculpted rocks, waterfalls small and large, whirlpools and a glittering glowworm grotto in its inner reaches. Real Journeys runs 2¼-hour guided tours, reaching the heart of the caves via a lake cruise, walkway and a short underground boat ride. Journeys depart from its office on Lakefront Dr.

🏃 Activities

Te Anau's **Lakeside Track** makes for a very pleasant stroll or cycle in either direction – north to the marina and around to the Upukerora River (around an hour return), or south past the Fiordland National Park Vis-itor Centre and on to the control gates and start of the Kepler Track (50 minutes).

☞ Tours

Fiordland Tours　　TOUR
(☑0800 247 249; www.fiordlandtours.co.nz; adult/child from $139/59) Runs small-group bus and Milford Sound cruise tours, departing from Te Anau and stopping at some interesting sights on the way. It also provides track transport and guided day walks on the Kepler Track.

Luxmore Jet　　JETBOATING
(☑0800 253 826; www.luxmorejet.com; Lakefront Dr; adult/child $99/49) One-hour trips on the Upper Waiau River (aka the River Anduin).

Southern Lakes Helicopters　　SCENIC FLIGHTS
(☑03-249 7167; www.southernlakeshelicopters. co.nz; Lakefront Dr) Flights over Te Anau for 30 minutes ($240), longer trips over Doubtful, Dusky and Milford Sounds (from $685), and various helihike, helibike and heliski options.

🛏 Sleeping

Te Anau Top 10　　HOLIDAY PARK **$**
(☑0800 249 746, 03-249 7462; www.teanautop10. co.nz; 128 Te Anau Tce; sites from $44, units from $129, without bathroom from $77; @🛜) Near the town and lake, this excellent, compact holiday park has private sites, a playground, lake-facing hot tubs, bike hire, a barbecue area and modern kitchen facilities. The mo-

tels units are very good indeed and there are well-priced cabins for those not bothered by communal bathrooms.

Te Anau YHA HOSTEL **$**
(☑ 03-249 7847; www.yha.co.nz; 29 Mokonui St; dm $34-39, s without bathroom $80-100, d with/without bathroom $105/96; @ ☎) This centrally located, modern hostel has great facilities and comfortable, colourful rooms. Play volleyball in the grassy backyard, crank up the barbecue or get cosy by the fire in the lounge.

Radfords on the Lake MOTEL **$$$**
(☑ 03-249 9186; www.radfordsonthelake.co.nz; 56 Lakefront Dr; units from $285; ☎) ✦ Radfords isn't your bog-standard motel, as you've probably already guessed by the grand-sounding name and commensurate prices. Set on manicured lawns across from the lake, this angular complex offers 14 luxurious units over two levels, all angled towards the view. They all have kitchens and five of them have spa baths.

Te Anau Lodge B&B **$$$**
(☑ 03-249 7477; www.teanaulodge.com; 52 Howden St; s/d from $210/240; ☎) The former 1930s-built Sisters of Mercy Convent, relocated to just north of town, offers an old-fashioned ambience with decor to match. Sip your complimentary wine in a chesterfield in front of the fire, retire to your spa bath before collapsing on a king-

size bed, then awaken to a fresh, delicious breakfast in the old chapel.

Eating

★ **Miles Better Pies** FAST FOOD **$**
(☑ 03-249 9044; www.milesbetterpies.co.nz; 19 Town Centre; pies $5-6.50; ☺ 6am-3pm) The bumper selection includes venison, lamb and mint, and fruit pies. There are a few pavement tables, but sitting and munching beside the lake is nicer.

Sandfly Cafe CAFE **$**
(☑ 03-249 9529; 9 The Lane; mains $7-20; ☺ 7am-4.30pm; ☎) Clocking the most local votes for the town's best espresso, simple but satisfying Sandfly is a top spot to enjoy an all-day breakfast, soup, sandwich or sweet treat, while listening to cruisy music or sunning yourself on the lawn.

★ **Redcliff Cafe** MODERN NZ **$$$**
(☑ 03-249 7431; www.theredcliff.co.nz; 12 Mokonui St; mains $38-42; ☺ 4-10pm) Housed in a replica settler's cottage, relaxed Redcliff offers generous fine-dining in a convivial atmosphere backed by sharp service. The predominantly locally sourced food is truly terrific: try the wild venison or hare. Kick off or wind it up with a drink in the rustic front bar, which often hosts live music.

Drinking & Entertainment

Ranch Bar & Grill PUB
(☑ 03-249 8801; www.theranchbar.co.nz; 111 Town Centre; ☺ noon-late) Popular with locals for its generous pub meals; head to the Ranch for a quality Sunday roast dinner ($15), Thursday jam night or a big sports match.

Fat Duck BAR
(☑ 03-249 8480; 124 Town Centre; ☺ noon-late Tue-Sun; ☎) This corner bar with pavement seating is a sound choice for supping a pint or two of Mac's beer. The kitchen dishes up marginally trendy gastropub and cafe fare, opening for breakfast daily in summer.

Fiordland Cinema CINEMA
(☑ 03-249 8812; www.fiordlandcinema.co.nz; 7 The Lane; ☎) In between back-to-back showings of the excellent *Ata Whenua/Fiordland on Film* (adult/child $10/5), essentially a 32-minute advertisement for Fiordland scenery, Fiordland Cinema serves as the local movie house. The **Black Dog Bar** (☑ 03-249 8844; www.blackdogbar.co.nz; ☺ 10am-

ESSENTIAL FIORDLAND & SOUTHLAND

Eat Bluff oysters, a New Zealand gourmet obsession.

Drink Craft beers brewed by Invercargill Brewery.

Read The poems of Hone Tuwhare (1922–2008), the most famous son of the Catlins.

Listen to The roar of waterfalls on the road to Milford Sound.

Watch *The World's Fastest Indian* (2005), for an understanding of Invercargill's deep devotion to the legacy of Burt Munro.

Online www.fiordland.org.nz, www.southlandnz.com, www.southernscenicroute.co.nz, www.stewartisland.co.nz

Area code ☑ 03

Te Anau

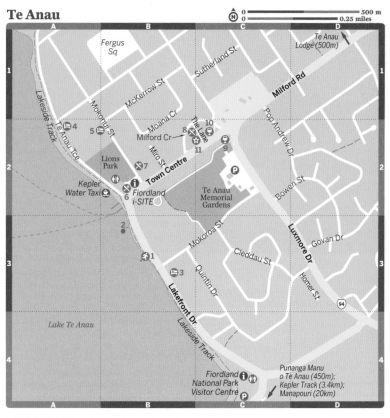

Te Anau

🏃 Activities, Courses & Tours
1 Luxmore Jet	B3
2 Southern Lakes Helicopters	B3

🛏 Sleeping
3 Radfords on the Lake	B3
4 Te Anau Top 10	A2
5 Te Anau YHA	A2

🍴 Eating
6 Miles Better Pies	B2

7 Redcliff Cafe	B2
8 Sandfly Cafe	B2

🍸 Drinking & Nightlife
Black Dog Bar	(see 11)
9 Fat Duck	C2
10 Ranch Bar & Grill	C2

🎭 Entertainment
11 Fiordland Cinema	C2

late; 🕾) downstairs is the town's most so-phisticated watering hole.

ℹ Information

Fiordland i-SITE (📞 03-249 8900; www.fiord land.org.nz; 19 Town Centre; ⏰ 8.30am-7pm Dec-Mar, to 5.30pm Apr-Nov) Activity, accom-modation and transport bookings.

Fiordland Medical Centre (📞 03-249 7007; 25 Luxmore Dr; ⏰ 8am-5.30pm Mon-Fri, 9am-noon Sat)

Fiordland National Park Visitor Centre (DOC; 📞 03-249 7924; www.doc.govt.nz; cnr Lake-front Dr & Te Anau–Manapouri Rd; ⏰ 8.30am-4.30pm) Can assist with Great Walks bookings, general hut tickets and information, with the bonus of a natural history display, and a shop

Kayaking, Milford Sound
IPGGUTENBERGUKLTD/GETTY IMAGES ©

stocking tramping supplies and essential topographical maps for backcountry trips.

Milford Sound

 Activities

Rosco's Milford Kayaks   KAYAKING
See p61

Descend Scubadiving   DIVING
(www.descend.co.nz; 2 dives incl gear $299) De-
scend runs day trips with four hours of cruis-
ing on Milford Sound in a 7m catamaran and
two dives along the way. The marine reserve
is home to unique marine life, including a
multitude of corals. Transport, equipment,
hot drinks and snacks are supplied.

 Tours

Cruise Milford   BOAT TOUR
(☑0800 645 367; www.cruisemilfordnz.com;
adult/child from $80/18; ☺10.45am, 12.45pm &

2.45pm) A small boat heads out three times
a day on a 1¾-hour cruise.

Real Journeys   BOAT TOUR
(☑0800 656 501, 03-249 7416; www.realjourneys.
co.nz) ✎ Milford's biggest operator runs various trips, including the popular 1¾-hour
scenic cruise (adult/child from $76/22).
The 2½-hour nature cruise (adult/child
from $88/22) hones in on wildlife with a
specialist nature guide providing commentary. Overnight cruises are also available, on
which you can kayak and take nature tours
in small boats en route.

🛏 Sleeping

Milford Sound Lodge   LODGE $$$
(☑03-249 8071; www.milfordlodge.com; SH94;
sites from $25, dm/d without bathroom $35/99,
chalets $345-395; ☏) Alongside the Cleddau
River, 1.5km from the Milford hub, this sim-
ple but comfortable lodge has a down-to-
earth, active vibe. Travellers and trampers
commune in the lounge or on-site Pio Pio
Cafe, which provides meals, wine and es-
presso. Luxurious chalets enjoy an absolute
riverside location. Booking ahead is strongly
recommended.

❶ Information

Discover Milford Sound Information Centre
(☑03-249 7931; www.southerndiscoveries.
co.nz; ☺8am-4pm) Although it's run by
Southern Discoveries, this centre near the
main car park sells tickets for most of the tour
and cruise companies, as well as for scenic
flights and InterCity buses. There's also a cafe
attached.

❶ Getting There & Away

CAR
Fill up with petrol in Te Anau before setting off.
Snow chains must be carried on ice- and ava-
lanche-risk days from May to November (there
will be signs on the road), and can be hired from
service stations in Te Anau.

Driving in New Zealand

New Zealand crams diversity into its island borders, and road journeys seamlessly combine ocean-fringed coastal roads, soaring alpine peaks and impressive glaciers.

Driving Fast Facts

➡ **Right or left?** Drive on the left

➡ **Manual or automatic?** Mostly automatic

➡ **Legal driving age** 18

➡ **Top speed limit** 100km/h

➡ **Best bumper sticker** 'Sweet as bro'

DRIVING LICENCE & DOCUMENTS

International visitors can use their home country driving licence, or an International Driving Permit (IDP) issued by their home country's automobile association. If their home country licence is not in English, they must also carry an approved translation of the licence. See www.nzta.govt.nz/driver-licences.

INSURANCE

Rental car companies include basic insurance in hire agreements, but it's often worth paying an additional fee – usually on a per day basis – to reduce your excess. This will bring the amount you need to pay in case of an accident down from around $1500 or $2000 to around $200 or $300. Note that most insurance agreements won't cover the cost of damage to glass (including the windscreen) or tyres, and insurance coverage is often invalidated on beaches and certain rough (4WD) unsealed roads. Always read the fine print and ask pertinent questions.

HIRING A CAR

Hiring a vehicle is very popular in NZ, and the country is perfect for self-drive adventures. Most – but not all – rental car companies require drivers to be at least 21 years old. The main companies are all represented; the following are good-value independent operators with national networks.

Ace Rental Cars (☎09-303 3112, ☎0800 502 277; www.acerentalcars.co.nz)

Apex Rentals (☎03-363 3000, ☎0800 500 660; www.apexrentals.co.nz)

Go Rentals (☎09-974 1598, ☎0800 467 368; www.gorentals.co.nz)

Also very popular is renting a campervan and taking advantage of the network of Department of Conservation (DOC) campsites. The following are three well-regarded local companies.

Apollo (☎09-889 2976, ☎0800 113 131; www.apollocamper.co.nz)

Jucy (☎09-929 2462, ☎0800 399 736; www.jucy.co.nz)

Road Trip Websites

AUTOMOBILE ASSOCIATIONS

New Zealand Automobile Association (www.aa.co.nz/travel) Provides emergency breakdown services, maps and accommodation guides.

CONDITIONS & TRAFFIC

New Zealand Transport Agency (www.nzta.govt.nz/traffic) Advice on roadworks, road closures and potential delays.

ROAD RULES

Drive Safe (www.drivesafe.org.nz) A simplified version of NZ's road rules, with the information of most interest to international visitors.

New Zealand Transport Agency (www.nzta.govt.nz) Search for 'Road Code' for the full version of NZ's road rules.

Maui (☎09-255 3910, ☎0800 688 558; www.maui.co.nz)

Another option is to contact **Transfer-car** (☎09-630 7533; www.transfercar.co.nz), one-way relocation specialists for car rental.

BUYING A VEHICLE IN NEW ZEALAND

Buying a car then selling it at the end of your travels can be one of the cheapest ways to see NZ.

➡ Auckland is the easiest place to buy a car, followed by Christchurch. **Turners Auctions** (www.turners.co.nz) is NZ's biggest car-auction operator, with 10 locations.

➡ Make sure your prospective vehicle has a Warrant of Fitness (WoF) and registration valid for a reasonable period: see the New Zealand Transport Agency website (www.nzta.govt.nz) for details.

➡ Buyers should take out third-party insurance, covering the cost of repairs to another vehicle resulting from an accident that is your fault: try the **Automobile Association** (AA; ☎0800 500 444; www.aa.co.nz/travel).

➡ To have a car inspected before you purchase it (around $150), see **Vehicle Inspection New Zealand** (VINZ; ☎09-573 3230, ☎0800 468 469; www.vinz.co.nz) or the AA.

➡ To establish if there's anything dodgy about the car (eg stolen, outstanding debts), try the AA's **LemonCheck** (☎09-420 3090, ☎0800 536 662; www.lemoncheck.co.nz) service.

BRINGING YOUR OWN VEHICLE

As NZ is an island nation, it is extremely rare for travellers to bring their own vehicle to the country. One exception where it could be financially worthwhile is for Australian visitors who are planning on travelling in their own campervan or caravan. Search for 'Importing a Vehicle Temporarily' on www.nzta.govt.nz.

MAPS

➡ Excellent national and regional maps published by the **New Zealand Automobile Association** (www.aa.co.nz) are available free of charge at regional i-SITEs (tourist information centres) and at main international airports. Also free and available at i-SITEs are regional maps and guides published by **Jasons** (www.jasons.co.nz).

➡ More detailed maps including street and topographic information are published by **Land Information New Zealand** (LINZ; www.linz.govt.nz).

➡ The Automobile Association also has a good online **Travel Time and Distance Calculator** to plan driving routes around NZ.

ROADS & CONDITIONS

➡ Kiwi traffic is usually pretty light, but it's easy to get stuck behind a slow-moving truck or a line of campervans. Be patient.

➡ One-way bridges, winding routes and unsealed gravel roads all require a more cautious driving approach.

➡ Carry tyre chains with you if you're travelling in alpine areas or over high passes during autumn and winter.

Road Distances (km), South Island

	Blenheim	Christchurch	Dunedin	Franz Josef Glacier	Greymouth	Invercargill	Kaikoura	Milford Sound	Nelson	Picton	Queenstown	Te Anau
Christchurch	310											
Dunedin	665	360										
Franz Josef Glacier	500	390	560									
Greymouth	330	250	550	180								
Invercargill	870	570	210	530	710							
Kaikoura	130	185	535	540	330	745						
Milford Sound	1060	760	410	630	805	275	930					
Nelson	115	425	775	470	290	990	245	1100				
Picton	30	340	690	530	355	900	160	1090	120			
Queenstown	785	480	285	355	530	190	660	290	820	815		
Te Anau	945	640	295	515	690	160	815	120	980	975	170	
Timaru	465	165	200	490	350	410	340	605	580	495	330	490

➡ If you stop for a photo, pull well over to the left and ensure your vehicle is not in the way of traffic.

➡ Distances on the map can be deceptive as narrow roads are often slower going than expected. Allow enough time for travel, and in more remote areas, ask at local petrol stations about the road ahead.

➡ Animal hazards often include farmers moving herds of cows or flocks of sheep. Slow your vehicle to a crawl – you may need to stop altogether – and patiently let the animals move around your car.

➡ Because of Auckland's geographic location, squeezed into a narrow coastal isthmus, rush-hour motorway traffic from 7am to 9am and 4pm to 7pm can be very slow. If possible, try and avoid heading north or south out of the city around these times.

ROAD RULES

The full version of New Zealand's road code can be found on www.nzta.govt.nz, but here are the basics:

➡ Drive on the left, overtake on the right.

➡ Safety belts (seat belts) must be worn by the driver and all passengers. Younger children must be secured in an approved child seat (these can be rented from rental-car companies).

➡ Motorcyclists and their passengers must always wear helmets.

➡ When entering a roundabout (traffic circle), always give way to the right.

➡ Come to a complete halt at STOP signs.

➡ The speed limit is 100km/h on motorways and the open road, and usually 50km/h in towns and cities. Always drive to the conditions and reduce speed if it is raining, windy or icy.

➡ For drivers over 20 years of age, the legal alcohol limit is 50mg of alcohol per 100mL of blood. This equates to around one to two standard drinks, but as different people process alcohol differently it is recommended that drivers should not drink at all. In NZ, drivers under the age of 20 cannot legally drink any alcohol if they are planning on driving.

➡ Driving under the influence of drugs is strictly illegal.

Road Distances (km), North Island

	Auckland	Cape Reinga	Hamilton	Napier	New Plymouth	Paihia	Rotorua	Taupo	Tauranga	Thames	Waitomo Caves
Cape Reinga	430										
Hamilton	125	555									
Napier	420	860	300								
New Plymouth	360	790	240	410							
Paihia	225	220	340	645	590						
Rotorua	235	670	110	220	300	460					
Taupo	280	720	155	140	300	505	80				
Tauranga	210	635	110	300	330	435	85	155			
Thames	115	540	110	360	340	345	170	210	115		
Waitomo Caves	200	620	75	300	180	420	165	170	150	175	
Wellington	640	1080	520	320	350	860	450	375	530	590	460

PARKING

➡ In city centres, most on-street parking is by 'pay and display' tickets available from on-street machines.

➡ Timing for paid parking is usually from 9am to 6pm Monday to Saturday with free parking on Sundays. This does vary in larger urban centres, however, so always check times carefully.

➡ Cash is needed for machines in provincial towns, but most city machines can also be paid by credit card or by smartphone.

➡ See www.wilsonparking.co.nz for locations of paid multistorey and underground car parks in Auckland, Hamilton, Wellington, Christchurch, Queenstown, Invercargill and Dunedin.

➡ Yellow lines along the edge of the road indicate a nonparking area, and drivers should also be aware of 'loading zones' which can only be used by commercial vehicles for short time periods.

➡ Clamping of vehicles is not very common in NZ, but council parking wardens and tow-truck drivers strictly enforce local parking rules – tow-away warnings should definitely be taken seriously.

FUEL

➡ Fuel is readily available throughout the country.

➡ See www.aa.co.nz/cars/motoring-blog/petrolwatch for current petrol and diesel prices.

➡ Fuel prices are generally cheaper in cities than in provincial areas.

➡ Most supermarkets offer fuel discount vouchers with shopping purchases over $40; check your docket.

SAFETY

➡ Driving in NZ is generally a hassle-free experience, but it is not unknown for rental cars and campervans to be targeted by opportunistic thieves.

➡ Always keep baggage and valuables locked in the back of the vehicle, out of sight. When parking in unattended car parks in popular tourist spots, consider carrying passports, money and other valuable items with you while you are away from your vehicle.

➡ If you have just arrived in the country after a long international flight, it is strongly recom-

mended that you have a re-energising overnight stay in your city of arrival before getting behind the wheel on NZ roads.

➡ **DriveSafe** (www.drivesafe.org.nz) is an excellent online resource – published in English, French, German and Chinese – for international drivers on NZ roads.

DOC CAMPSITES & FREEDOM CAMPING

A great option for campervan travellers are the 250-plus vehicle-accessible 'Conservation Campsites' run by the Department of Conservation (www.doc.govt.nz). Fees range from free (basic toilets and fresh water) to $15 per adult (flush toilets and showers). Pick up brochures detailing every campsite from DOC offices and i-SITEs or see online.

New Zealand is so photogenic, it's often tempting to just pull off the road and camp for the night, but there are strict guidelines for 'freedom camping'. See www.camping.org.nz for more freedom-camping tips.

➡ Never assume it's OK to camp somewhere: always ask a local or check with the local i-SITE, DOC office or commercial camping ground.

➡ If you are freedom camping, treat the area with respect and do not leave any litter.

➡ If your chosen campsite doesn't have toilet facilities and neither does your campervan, it's illegal for you to sleep there (your campervan must also have an on-board grey-water storage system).

➡ Legislation allows for $200 instant fines for camping in prohibited areas or improper disposal of waste (in cases where dumping waste could damage the environment, fees are up to $10,000).

RADIO

New Zealand is well covered by radio, and national station networks can be listened to on different frequencies around the country. Check each network's website for the relevant frequency in various areas of the country.

Radio New Zealand National (www.radionz.co.nz/national) News-oriented station

Driving Problem-Buster

What should I do if my car breaks down? Call the service number of your car-hire company and a local garage will be contacted. If you're travelling in your own vehicle, join the New Zealand Automobile Association (www.aa.co.nz); they can attend to breakdowns day and night. Another option is Motoring 24-7 (www.roadside-assistance.co.nz).

What if I have an accident? Exchange basic information with the other party (name, insurance details, driving licence number). No discussion of liability needs to take place at the scene. It's a good idea to photograph the scene of the accident noting key details. Call the police (☑111) if necessary.

What should I do if I get stopped by the police? They will want to see your driving licence, and a valid form of ID if you are visiting from overseas. Breath testing is mandatory in NZ.

What if I can't find anywhere to stay? Try to book ahead during busy periods. Local i-SITEs can often help with last-minute accommodation bookings.

Will I need to pay tolls in advance? New Zealand has three toll roads on the North Island: the Northern Gateway Toll Road north of Auckland, and the Tauranga Eastern Link Toll Road and the Takitimu Drive Toll Road, both in Tauranga. Tolls are specific to a vehicle's registration number and can be paid online at www.nzta.govt.nz or at Caltex and BP service stations. Tolls can be paid either prior to travel, or within five days of travelling on a specific toll road.

Cruising Cook Strait

On a clear day, sailing into Wellington Harbour, or into Picton in the Marlborough Sounds, is magical. Cook Strait can be rough, but the big ferries handle it well, and distractions include cafes, bars and cinemas. Booking online is easiest; sailings can usually be booked up to a couple of days in advance. Exceptions are during school and public holidays, and from late December to the end of January. There are two ferry options:

Bluebridge Ferries (☎04-471 6188, 0800 844 844; www.bluebridge.co.nz; 50 Waterloo Quay) Crossing takes 3½ hours; up to four sailings in each direction daily. Bluebridge is based at Waterloo Quay, opposite Wellington train station.

Interislander (☎04-498 3302, 0800 802 802; www.interislander.co.nz; Aotea Quay) Crossings take three hours, 10 minutes; up to five sailings in each direction daily. Interislander is about 2km northeast of Wellington's centre at Aotea Quay.

Car-hire companies allow you to pickup/drop off vehicles at ferry terminals. If you arrive outside business hours, arrangements can be made to collect your vehicle from the terminal car park. In some cases, it may suit the hire company for you to take your rental car with you on the ferry – eg for relocations etc – so ask them to advise what will be the best deal.

with excellent coverage of local issues, arts and culture.

Newstalk ZB (www.newstalkzb.co.nz) Talkback station where the issues of the day are discussed passionately.

Radio Sport (www.radiosport.co.nz) Understand the difference between the All Blacks, Black Caps and Silver Ferns (respectively NZ's national rugby, cricket and netball teams).

Hauraki (www.hauraki.co.nz) Iconic rock music station with a quintessentially irreverent Kiwi tone.

BEHIND THE SCENES

SEND US YOUR FEEDBACK

We love to hear from travellers – your comments help make our books better. We read every word, and we guarantee that your feedback goes straight to the authors. Visit **lonelyplanet. com/contact** to submit your updates and suggestions.

Note: We may edit, reproduce and incorporate your comments in Lonely Planet products such as guidebooks, websites and digital products, so let us know if you don't want your comments reproduced or your name acknowledged. For a copy of our privacy policy visit lonelyplanet.com/privacy.

ACKNOWLEDGMENTS

Climate map data adapted from Peel MC, Finlayson BL & McMahon TA (2007) 'Updated World Map of the Köppen-Geiger Climate Classification', *Hydrology and Earth System Sciences*, 11, 163344.

Cover photographs: Front: Road leading to Lake Tekapo and Aoraki/Mt Cook, eye35.pix/Alamy©; Back: Queenstown, Apexphotos/Getty©

THIS BOOK

This 1st edition of *New Zealand's South Island Road Trips* was researched and written by Brett Atkinson, Sarah Bennett, Peter Dragicevich and Lee Slater. This guidebook was produced by the following:

Destination Editor Tasmin Waby

Product Editor Alison Ridgway

Senior Cartographer Diana Von Holdt

Book Designer Virginia Moreno

Assisting Editors Bruce Evans, Gabrielle Stefanos

Assisting Cartographers Corey Hutchison

Assisting Book Designers Michael Buick, Katherine Marsh, Wendy Wright

Cover Researcher Naomi Parker

Thanks to Grace Dobell, Andi Jones, Catherine Naghten, Kirsten Rawlings, Kathryn Rowan

OUR STORY

A beat-up old car, a few dollars in the pocket and a sense of adventure. In 1972 that's all Tony and Maureen Wheeler needed for the trip of a lifetime – across Europe and Asia overland to Australia. It took several months, and at the end – broke but inspired – they sat at their kitchen table writing and stapling together their first travel guide, *Across Asia on the Cheap*. Within a week they'd sold 1500 copies. Lonely Planet was born.

Today, Lonely Planet has offices in Dublin, Franklin, London, Melbourne, Oakland, Beijing and Delhi, with more than 600 staff and writers. We share Tony's belief that 'a great guidebook should do three things: inform, educate and amuse'.

INDEX

A

Abel Tasman National Park 24
accommodation 13, *see also individual locations*
Aoraki/Mt Cook 46
Aoraki/Mt Cook National Park 45-7, 93-5, **94-5**
Arthur's Pass 89-90
Arthur's Pass National Park 39-40, 89

B

Bannockburn 44
Blenheim 26, 30-2, 67-9
breakdown services 118
breweries
    Christchurch 87-8
    Mapua 77
    Motueka 78
    Waipara Valley 88-9
    Wanaka 102
bungy jumping 97

C

campervans 117-18
camping 121
canoeing & kayaking
    Blenheim 68
    Christchurch 82
    Havelock 67
    Milford Sound 61
    Tasman Glacier 93
car hire 117-18
car insurance 117
car travel, *see* driving
Cascade Creek 57
caves 53-4, 113
cell phones 12
Chasm Creek 60
Christchurch 10, 34, 39, 81-8, **84-5**
    accommodation 83
    activities 82-3
    drinking & nightlife 87
    food 86-7
    shopping 87
    sights 81-2
    tours 83
churches & cathedrals
    Christ Church Cathedral 74
    Transitional Cathedral 82
climate 12
Cook Strait 122
costs 13
Cromwell 44-5, 106-7
    accommodation 107
    activities 106
    festivals & events 107
    food 107
    sights 106-7
Cullen Point Lookout 66

D

Department of Conservation (DOC) 121
Devil's Staircase 53
Divide, the 57-8
diving 64
documents 117
driving 117-22
    car buying 118
    car hire 117-18
    documents 117
    fuel 12, 120
    insurance 117
    maps 118
    parking 120
    road rules 118, 119
    safety 118-19, 120-1
    websites 118
driving licences 117

E

emergencies 12, 118

F

ferry travel 122
Fiordland 113-16
Fiordland National Park 58
food 13, 21, *see also individual locations*
Fox Glacier 41, 110-12, **111**
    accommodation 111

000 Map pages

activities 110
  food 112
freedom camping 121
fuel 12, 120

G

gas 12, 120
Geraldine 48-9, 91
Gore Bay 32-3
greenstone 40

H

Havelock 19, 66-7
helicopter tours 46, 92, 113
heliskiing 93
Highlands Motorsport Park 45-6
highlights 8-9
hiking, *see* walking
Hokitika 40, 108-10, **109**
  accommodation 109
  activities 108-9
  drinking 110
  food 110
  sights 108
Hokitika Gorge 108
Homer Tunnel 58-60
horse riding 91
hot springs 91

I

insurance 117
International Antarctic Centre 39
internet access 12

J

jetboating 44, 97

K

Kaikoura 9, 32, 70-4, **72**
Kaikoura Coast 29-35

kayaking, *see* canoeing & kayaking
kiwis 96

L

Lake Gunn 57
Lake Kaniere 108
Lake Mistletoe 54
Lake Tekapo 47-8, 91-2
Lake Wakatipu 96

M

Mackay Creek 54-5
Mackenzie Country 47
Makarora 43-4, 105-6
  activities 105-6
maps 118
Mapua 77
Marlborough 64-80
Marlborough Sounds 20
Marlborough Wine Region 26, 70-1, **68**
Mavora Lakes 54
Methven 49, 90-1
Milford Sound 9, 51-61, 116
Mirror Lakes 55-7
Mitre Peak 55
mobile phones 12
money 13
motorsports 106
Motueka 23-4, 78-9, **79**
Moutere Hills 77-8
Mt Aspiring National Park 45
museums & galleries
  Canterbury Museum 34, 82
  Christchurch Art Gallery 81
  Edwin Fox Maritime Museum 64
  Geraldine Museum 91
  Höglund Art Glass 77
  Hokitika Museum 108
  Kaikoura Museum 70

  Marlborough Museum 67
  Motueka District Museum 78
  National Transport & Toy Museum 102
  Nelson Provincial Museum 74
  Picton Museum 64
  Quake City 82
  Sir Edmund Hillary Alpine Centre 93
  Suter Art Gallery 74
  Vintage Car & Machinery Museum 91-2
  World of WearableArt Museum 20
music 121

N

national parks & reserves
  Abel Tasman National Park 24
  Aoraki/Mt Cook National Park 45-7, 93-5, **94-5**
  Arthur's Pass National Park 39-40, 89
  Fiordland National Park 58
  Mt Aspiring National Park 45
  Nelson Lakes National Park 24-5, 79-80
Nelson 20-1, 74-7, **75**
Nelson Lakes National Park 24-5, 79-80

P

parking 120
parks & gardens, *see also* national parks & reserves
  Christchurch Botanic Gardens 81
  Hagley Park 81
  Queenstown Gardens 53
Pelorus Bridge 19-20
petrol 12, 120

Picton 19, 30, 64-6, **65**
pounamu 40

Q

Queenstown 9, 11, 44, 53, 96-101, **98**
　accommodation 98-9
　activities 97
　drinking & nightlife 100
　entertainment 101
　food 99-100
　shopping 101-2
　sights 96-7
　tours 97-8
Queenstown Gardens 53

R

radio 121-2
Rakaia Gorge 49
Renwick 25
road distances 119, 120
road rules 118, 119
Ross 40-1
Ross Goldfields Heritage Centre 40

S

safety 118-19, 120-1
sandflies 41
seals 70
Ship Creek 41-3
Siberia Experience 43-4
skiing 48, 90, 93
skydiving
　Fox Glacier 110
　Methven 90
　Motueka 24, 78

snowboarding 48
Southern Alps 37-49
Southland 113-16

T

Talbot Forest Scenic Reserve 48
Tasman Glacier 93
Te Anau 53-4, 113-16, **115**
　accommodation 113-14
　activities 113
　drinking & nightlife 114-15
　food 114
　sights 113
　tours 113
Te Anau Glowworm Caves 53-4
telephone services 12
tipping 13
tramping, *see* walking
transport 13

U

Upper Moutere 21-3, 77

W

Waimea Estate 21
Waipara Valley 33-4, 88-9
walking
　Arthur's Pass 89
　Blue Pools Walk 105
　Bridle Track 105
　Fox Glacier 110
　Gillespie Pass 106
　Haast Pass Lookout Track 105
　Havelock 67

Hooker Valley Track 93
Kaikoura 70
Kea Point Track 93
Sealy Tarns Track 93
Tasman Glacier 93
Wilkin Valley Track 106
Wanaka 44, 101-5, **103**
　accommodation 102-4
　activities 102
　drinking & nightlife 104
　entertainment 105-6
　food 104
　shopping 105
　sights 101-2
　tours 102
weather 12
websites 13, 118
West Coast 108-12
whales 34
white-water rafting
　Kaikoura 71
　Queenstown 97
wi-fi 12
wildlife parks & reserves
　Kiwi Birdlife Park 96
　Point Kean Seal Colony 70
　Punanga Manu o Te Anau 113
wildlife watching 34
wineries
　Bannockburn 44
　Blenheim 31
　Marlborough 26, 70-1
　Mt Difficulty 107
　Nelson 21
　Waipara Valley 34, 88
　Wanaka 102

OUR WRITERS

BRETT ATKINSON

Born in Rotorua, and now resident in Auckland, Brett has been tripping around New Zealand for most of his life. He has ventured to sleepy harbours in Northland and negotiated coastal roads around Coromandel. Together with his wife, Carol, he's explored many countries independently behind the wheel of a car.

PETER DRAGICEVICH

After nearly a decade working for off-shore publishing companies, Peter's life has come full circle, returning to his home city of Auckland. As Managing Editor of *Express* newspaper he spent much of the '90s writing about the local arts, club and bar scene. After dozens of Lonely Planet assignments, writing about New Zealand remains his favourite gig.

SARAH BENNETT

Sarah grew up in Marlborough, but her life-long love affair with Wellington has left her loyalties divided between North and South. What is constant is her obsession with NZ road trips, which keeps her and husband, Lee, on the road in their little campervan for around four months each year. Their mountain bikes always come with them, as do hiking boots, a hot-water bottle and the laptop (of course) because it's not always sunshine and wine.

LEE SLATER

Lee embarked on his first NZ road trip just after moving there from the UK in 1999. What soon became blindingly obvious was the difference between the two country's roads. Swapping 20-mile traffic jams on multilaned highways for empty, winding roads that cut through some of the world's most impressive scenery has been a tough job. Upgrading from pup tent to campervan with his beau, Sarah Bennett, has softened the blow somewhat.

Published by Lonely Planet Global Limited
CRN 554153
1st edition – December 2016
ISBN 978 1 78657 195 3
© Lonely Planet 2016   Photographs © as indicated 2016
10 9 8 7 6 5 4 3 2 1
Printed in China